ELEMENTAL ABUNDANCE

Be the light

with Love

Iona

The 4 keys to Unlocking Your Full Hearted Life

By Iona Russell

DEDICATION

This book is dedicated to my mum who is always with me in Spirit, my dad who has been a mirror and my son who is my biggest teacher.

But above all, to all of You, who are so innately Powerful, so Elementally Abundant, you do not know it yet. You are soon to discover as I did, what is truly possible, once you understand the power of the Elemental Forces that are available to you.

CONTENTS

Introduction   7

Foreword 1 by Niyc Pidgeon   9

Foreword 2 by Richard Knight   13

PART 1 - THE BEGINNING OF THE BEGINNING   17

Chapter 1: My Story   19

Chapter 2: The Elemental Structure   27

Chapter 3: How to Use This Book   31

Chapter 4: Preparing Yourself for the Journey   33

Chapter 5: Reflections & Suggestions: The Beginning of the Beginning   41

PART 2 - EARTH: THE FOUNDATIONS OF LIFE   45

Chapter 6: The Earth Principle   47

Earth Step 1: Ground Thyself   51

Chapter 7: As Above, So Below   53

Chapter 8: The Power of Being in Nature   57

Chapter 9: Learning to Fly   61

Chapter 10 : Reflections & Suggestions: Ground Thyself   65

Earth Step 2: Know Thyself   69

Chapter 11: Living With Joy, Love, and Gratitude   71

Chapter 12: Embodied Emotional Health   77

Chapter 13: Intuition   85

Chapter 14: Personal Values to Empower You   95

Chapter 15: Reflections & Suggestions: Know Thyself   103

PART 3 - WATER: REFLECTION   107

Chapter 16: The Water Principle   109
Chapter 17: Thoughts and Beliefs   113
Chapter 18: Messages from the Past   129
Chapter 19: Forgiveness   137
Chapter 20 : Reflections & Suggestions: Water Element   141

PART 4 - AIR: INTENTION, DIRECTION & FLOW   145

Chapter 21: The Air Principle   147
Chapter 22: Live Your Vision, Live Your Legacy   155
Chapter 23: The Best Version of You   159
Chapter 26: Reflections & Suggestions:Air Element   163

PART 5 - FIRE: ALIGNMENT   167

Chapter 27: The Fire Principle   169
Chapter 28: Mining Your Fuel for the Fire   175
Chapter 29: Fanning the Flames with Action   183
Chapter 30: The Combustion = Fuel + Heart + Oxygen
(Igniting Your Why)   191
Chapter 31: The Final Key: The Elements in Harmony   199

Author Bio   204
Books by Iona Russell   206

INTRODUCTION

Hello Dear Elemental Reader

Now is your time to BE who you were born to BE; it is time for you to be Elementally Abundant. By working with the four elements of Earth, Water, Air and Fire, you can step into your highest power, your fullest embodiment, your most expansive and radiant self. Your truest nature: your natural Abundance.

I believe we are here to live fully, to see and access all the possibilities the Universe has to offer, in every area of our lives. That's our journey, our quest.

Think of this book as your 'Elemental' guide, a resource with proven techniques and exercises for you to create your Heart-Full Abundant life. Each technique and every practice is borne of my experience as an intuitive coach, a spiritual mentor, and my training in positive psychology. We'll bridge the Mind, Body, and Soul connection for YOUR Elemental Success. I know these principles and processes work because they have worked for me and for my clients, and I'm so excited to share them together in one place.

Just as certain elements were essential for life to occur on this beautiful planet, our four elements of Earth, Water, Air and Fire can be seen essential to our ongoing evolution and growth. We are one with nature, and when we bring the four elements into balance and fully integrate them into the way we live and the way we be, we create PURE Abundance from our Hearts, and it flows into all areas of our lives.

There is no other route to Pure Abundance. No shortcuts. And you wouldn't want there to be: because the journey is such a gift.

Being in alignment with the four elements means being in alignment with nature and natural flow. You'll discover I'm a nature junkie. It's where I am most alive, most connected to the abundance within me. I grew up in nature as a free-spirited hippie child in the 70's and it is to nature I return for inspiration, support, release, and connection to the Life Force of the Universe.

"Water soothes and heals. Air refreshes and revives. Earth grounds and holds. Fire is a burning reminder of our own will and creative power. Swallow their spells. There's a certain sweet comfort in knowing that you belong to them all."

- Victoria Erickson

The definition of an element is *that which cannot be broken down into a simpler substance*. The four elements are whole and complete, just as you are whole and complete. This journey will bring you back into balance and into the vibration of your Elemental Abundance.

To support you on your journey and to go deeper with these practices come and join the free Elemental Community Circle www.ionarussell.com/elemental-circle. You will find bonus material, PDF downloads, audio mediations, and videos from me to you, my dear creative elemental reader.

It is time for you to come back to your Elemental Abundance. Abundance in business, finance, health, relationships, creativity, gratitude, magic and creation.

You are an Elemental Being, about to reclaim your Abundance.

Welcome.

FOREWORD 1

by Niyc Pidgeon

"How good can I feel...? How easy can it be...?" These are two questions I ask daily to align my energy and remind myself of the gentle power of intention and to align with generosity in abundance.

Over the last many decades of being on a personal growth journey I've continued the process of deepening the connection with spirit and with myself.

Whether through the gentle whispers of intuition, or within the throes of challenge, all of our life experience is valid - and all is supporting our growth.

Walking a spiritual path affords us new levels of depth, understanding, and success, and even though the path isn't one that's always easy, within the depths and complexity of experience comes renewal, new evolution, and beautiful growth.

As an Award-Winning Positive Psychologist, Best-Selling Author, and Certified Coach, I've made it my life's work to help people live with more joy, personal power, and Unstoppable Success within themselves and their lives.

Whilst someone might initially decide to engage with my work because they want to experience more richness in their outer world, what ultimately happens is an unlocking and connection with the well of wealth inside.

Positive Psychology teaches us that it's possible to shift the way you feel in an instant, by raising your self awareness and choosing to pick up a proven tool - knowing that simple steps will also then compound over time to result in profound and lasting change.

Instead of focusing on what's going wrong in the world, or what is wrong with other people and ourselves, the science of happiness gets us to align with where we are strong, and focus on human strength and virtue instead.

Rather than seeing happiness as a goal somewhere out there in the future, you can understand it as a process that is ever unfolding - an adventure within which we get to meet ourselves every step of the way.

In the pages of *Elemental Abundance*, Iona is helping you do that as she shares from her own vast personal experience and embodiment of the modalities and practices she has developed and taught over her many years of commitment to doing the work.

Having worked closely with Iona for a long long time now I have witnessed - and I am in awe of - her continued dedication to both being in the work, and also being a conduit for the work - helping so many people through the integration of spiritual, shamanic, and scientific tools to bring forward big breakthroughs and access new levels of self.

You can trust that the tools shared within this book will not just help you grow, but will crack you open and help call you forward to feel more, experience more, and ultimately be more too.

I believe we are always the student, and are honoured to be so. The path of the student is a rich path!

We get to walk together, learn together, and to deepen in the process together - and when we recognise the process is in fact the reward, we realize we are living out our vision and are experiencing our next level right now.

This book will help you continue to commit to living with a sense of curiosity and exploration so you can open up new territory within your life, within your body, within your heart to be Elementally Abundant.

Our opportunity in this lifetime is to come back to ourselves, to remember the power and the truth of who we are, and this book will help you do exactly that.

With Gratitude,

Niyc Pidgeon

Positive Psychologist MSc IPPA, Hay House Author "Now Is Your Chance", Certified High Performance Coach, Founder Of Unstoppable Success, & Positive Psychology Coach Academy Certification.

FOREWORD 2

by Richard Knight

I envy you, dear reader, you are about to embark on a life-changing and magical journey to your Elementally Abundant Life. The book you are now holding will be your guide, your map to finding your true-life path with prosperity and purpose; and walking that authentic path. Walking this path with you is one of the world's leading Intuitive Coaches and a truly inspirational and magical human being.

I have had the pleasure of sharing the platform with Iona on several occasions. Using the techniques that she describes in this book, she can transform people's lives in minutes. You can literally see the change in their eyes when 'their destination and their Big Dream' comes into view for the first time.

Usually, when you write a foreword the expectation is that you review or summarise the contents of the book. I'm not going to. I have two reasons:

1. I don't want to spoil anything. You have so many 'lightbulb' moments and insights to discover. One tip: read with a pen and a journal in front of you. You will find yourself making a lot of notes.

2. I could never do justice to Iona's quirky and often hilarious writing, usually just before she delivers a spectacular 'truth bomb' or insight.

But I'll give you a heads up: read and then re-read Chapter 27, it will change your life.

I can give Iona, and indeed this book, no greater compliment than to say they are the 'real deal'. I have worked in this field for nearly 40 years and so much of the information out there is simply regurgitated from book to book or speaker to speaker.

If you've never met Iona (and you really should) she is a lady who 'walks the walk'. Her approach is built on her own transformational life experiences and on her work with hundreds of clients in the real world — and it works.

This is not a book of fanciful new-age mumbo jumbo, this is a grounded and practical approach to building and living your Big Dream... With maybe a sprinkling of fairy dust, because that's how Iona rolls.

I'll stop now, I'm going to delay you no longer. You have an amazing journey ahead of you with the most inspirational person I know.

Bon Voyage ...

Richard Knight

The World's Leading Psychic Medium, 'Mozart of modern tarot'

PART 1:

The Beginning of the Beginning

CHAPTER 1

My Story

"Plant seeds of happiness, hope, success, and love; it will all come back to you in abundance. This is the law of nature."

— *Steve Maraboli*

I lay there on the bed, alone with the tears of grief streaming down my face — THIS was not how it was supposed to be, not at 42!

This was one of those watershed moments: those moments where you draw a line in the sand and choose change — even when you have no idea how to initiate it, what it will look like, or where it will take you. Although I had begun the deep journey into finding myself and tuning into what I now call 'The Elements of Abundance' some three years earlier, this moment, at 42, was to become the catalyst for the realignment of my outer world.

But ... before I share more of my story, let me ask, do you believe you are capable of creating YOUR life of Abundance? Do you feel, as I did, that you're living a half-life, or even worse, a life of no value? That while you're playing at BE-ing THIS you, the real you is at a grand ball, dancing through life, loving every moment of discovery and adventure?

Do you seek that elusive sense of Ease and Prosperity, to know that each step on your path leads to a life of plenty?

There's a natural confidence that comes when you live the certainty of your own inner and outer Wealth, and the right people and opportunities come into your life when you walk your Prosperous Path. Are you ready to make a commitment to tune into the vibration of your Abundance?

I did, granted a little later in life maybe, but True change is never late; it arrives exactly when you're ready for it.

Finding my way 'home' to that part of me that saw my own true value, self worth and abundance in everything I already had, and the opportunities at my fingertips, after over 40 years of learning otherwise, was a raw experience, and one I began before I could even walk, let alone dance. This was the coming home to ME, to all that I am, a whole and complete being, Worthy, Powerful and *Abundant*.

You see, in a spiritual context, the notion of abundance is less about the limited material world outside of us, and everything to do with the infinite world within us.

The paradigm-shifting truth is we are all naturally abundant because through our Hearts we always have access to the bountiful and ever-generous spiritual domain.

Everything we feel lies within our heart, and we can tap into the fullness, the light, the perfection — in other words, the abundance of life and the universe — at any time.

I'll be taking you through processes to drop into your heart throughout the book, but right now I just want you to know that when I talk about living an abundant life, I'm inviting you to a way of being in the world that will naturally and effortlessly make you feel whole.

In abundance, you see only plenty. Your heart is full. Your soul expands. You're rooted, in flow, soaring and alight, all at once. You're elemental.

THE JOURNEY BACK TO MY HEART

When I was born, our family farm in rural South Wales was a mystical place. Not a traditional 'working farm' anymore, but a magical haven which acted like a magnetic pull to city-dwellers looking to escape the smog and connect with the land. An abundance of seekers, hippies, movie stars, mountain men, gypsies, sheep farmers, and spiritual leaders flowed through the farm and my childhood, colouring it and giving it life.

When I was seven years old, I was casually introduced to the 16th Karmapa, who blessed the farm and held ceremonies there along with his monks and followers. There were caravans, golden and red buses, tepees, and hippies gathering around campfires.

The picture I just painted is rosy, right? Indeed, the person I am today can look back on my early childhood and see most of it in all its crazy glory. I can feel appreciation for how myself and my family were a kaleidoscope of quirky effervescent ecstatic adventurers, then dancing across time to the rhythm of our own song. But soon, that dream was to be disrupted, and as a free-spirited child, I was ill-prepared for what was to come. Life, it seemed, had a different plan for me.

I was eight when my parents divorced and my mum, brothers, and I left that little slice of bohemia, and this marked the beginning of my light dimming. The transition was hard, and not fitting into 'normal' society meant that as adolescence loomed into view, I didn't get the sense of connection and support I needed.

Through my teenage years, I built a tower around my Heart, with shadowed wounds and dark corridors. By the time I reached fourteen, anorexia, bulimia, and an unhealthy appetite for hard spirits were the cornerstones of my young life. Not to mention the tell-tale appearance of scarred wrists that come with attempted suicides, telling any onlookers all they needed to know. I was lost!

So began my global search for satisfaction, which saw me living and working in Australia with my camper van, spending time in Hawaii where I fell in love with sky diving, backpacking through Europe, driving across the USA a few times, and embarking upon many adventures across Canada. They were crazy days filled with sensations and stimulation. They also masked the pain I felt inside.

Then, at 33 I became a mother to my greatest teacher, my son Callum. With that gift came the spectre of post-natal depression, which strained an already volatile relationship, and led to an uneasy breakup. I was growing tired of change and now sought solace in stability. Those crazy years of rebellion and wildness were both entertaining and made for great stories and friendship, but beneath them was the fragile scaffolding of my childhood, the pain, the sense of abandonment, and not belonging.

So, seven years later when I met and fell in love with a man who I'd go on to marry, it was both a surprise and a risk to me. But it was what I thought I was so desperately in need of: knowing there was someone there for me, for my son, for a future that could be structured and stable, but still with the hint of adventure as we moved to Texas.

We entered a committed relationship, with all the hopes and dreams of eternity, of having found 'The One', of it being forever. But, quite quickly, it became apparent that in the flush and rush of attraction (or was it more distraction), we'd not quite learned who we were as a couple, what our values were, or how we wanted life to look and feel with each other, and with my son.

I'm not going to play a blame game here, there are rarely pure innocents in any breakup, but it was a few short years into my marriage that I had that watershed moment. At the age of 42, I sat up in bed one night and cried, "I can't do this anymore."

My husband and I were lost in a cycle of toxicity and conflict. Something had to change, and even though I had declared I couldn't go on as we were, I didn't know what or how to create the change we so desperately needed. Divorce would come, only not just yet. First, I tried to mend and repair us, not realising that what was crying out for transformation was my Soul, and that was a journey I would take alone.

Until I could face that realisation, I remained in my marriage. Before long, I was clinically diagnosed with situational depression, and even more lost than before. I was adrift and directionless, in a void of not knowing who, or what, I was anymore. Reality was blurred, hidden amongst anxious careful conversations with my husband, each of us managing our misplaced expectations, and avoiding the truth. Everything unsaid and unexpressed fermented and the chasm between us grew as we both ignored the elephant crying in the corner. One thing was for sure – if I continued this way, I was heading towards a dark unrecoverable place filled with emptiness, lack and emotional poverty.

So began the real search, my search for Abundance in myself, and my life. I still had hope that when that rich sense of 'I have everything I need' was found, family normality could also be found, and my marriage might be saved.

I spent several months seeking and reaching out to what I felt was aligned to me. I found people with similar interests and gravitated toward those who were asking the same philosophical questions as I was at that time. I went to metaphysical meet-ups, tarot workshops, a workshop for intuitively creating your own oracle cards, art classes, philosophical discussion gatherings, and randomly joined a group that met to play mahjong (which it turns out I Loved).

I wanted to feel full of life, find the abundance, and find what I was looking for. The truth was, I *didn't know* what I was looking for, or who I was looking for, what 'Spiritual Abundance' was, or who to look for to help me find it — until I was eventually gifted the presence of a wonderful genuine Soul, an intuitive and beautiful guide, humble and so giving of herself. Her name was Madhavi, but even she was just the beginning, not the end.

For the next eighteen months, through the guidance of Madhavi, I immersed myself in the spiritual wisdoms and practices that would be the foundation of not only finding my self worth, but also recognising the Abundance already within me: the kindling that lit the fire of everything I have become since, to this beautiful bountiful and elementally abundant present day.

Had I found a land of constantly flowing milk and honey, where vast rivers of gold ran right into my bank account, and where my Emotional, Physical, and Spiritual cups ranneth over? Not quite, not yet, but thankfully I had found something far more valuable: the courage and conviction to deal with the greatest challenge of my life so far. The passing of my beautiful beloved mother, Maggie.

It was 24th November 2015 when she passed from her Earthly bond and returned home to her spirit place. I had not long returned from a trip from my native Scotland back to the States and no sooner had I landed than I whisked Callum and I to Halifax Nova Scotia to be with her in her final days.

It was hard, and beautiful at the same time, as my brothers and I remembered fondly, and mourned deeply as a family. We were all there: dear friends, extended family, partners, and grandchildren. Except that my husband wasn't there. He was working away and had been for a little while. And while I didn't see it or speak of it as an issue, in the darkness of the passing night, as the cold Canadian air whistled outside, I realised that despite the work I had done, I was yet again, alone.

This was my greatest realisation to date: that while we heal ourselves, and as we uncover our greatest wounds, we are exposed to our deepest and most important truths. We discover what we truly desire, what we no longer want, and what an Elementally Abundant life is uniquely, for us.

I had been living a double life. While my inner journey was deep and profound, my external world, the one of family, just wasn't functioning as it should. Three years after realising we couldn't carry on as we were, we realised we couldn't carry on at all. It was time to end the charade.

The conversations were difficult, as truth often is when heard for the first time. But eventually, we agreed with the inevitable and in May of 2016, Callum and I left the US and my husband, and began settling into our new home in my native Scotland. Yes, it was hard, as a single parent in a different (albeit familiar) country, having to start again... BUT, this time I had both my direction AND the knowledge and practices to handle anything. Not just handle, but actualise, materialise and realise the opportunities ahead of me.

So began, after all the lessons learned, and the gifts they now brought me, my return to True Abundance, my reconnection with my own Wealth Creation Life Source – the wellspring of Inner Power for me. I went from bleak lack consciousness to creating my dream life, and a significant part of that dream involves sharing with YOU all I now know in the hope that maybe, just maybe, I catch you before you fall too deeply into the shadows, and bring you up, up into your brightest light. Which brings me nicely to...

WHY THIS BOOK? WHY YOU? WHY NOW?

I'll tell you how I see it.

I believe it's your destiny to live a full and Abundant life. A life packed with potential, with connections and resources, and of course — unbridled fun, and the kind of experiences that only YOU can call into existence.

This is your journey, and your dance, after all.

I've created this book with the pure intention to be your guide, your Madhavi, towards Abundance being an Elemental source in your life, whatever that looks like for you.

I don't have your answers; because they're within you. I only want you to know that which you already know ... that which has been lost or is buried deep. Together, we will unearth and mine these buried treasures, reconnecting you powerfully to your unique Elemental wellspring of Abundance.

Next, let me tell you a little about each of the four elements, and the voyage we're about to take.

CHAPTER 2

The Elemental Structure

"The goal of life is to make your heartbeat match the beat of the universe, to match your nature with Nature."

— *Joseph Campbell*

The foundations of the processes I'll share on these pages align with the elements of EARTH, WATER, AIR, and FIRE. We'll use them to break through the doors of perception so you can come on this transformational journey with me, breaking through your limits, and powerfully manifesting your beautiful Elemental Abundant Life.

EARTH represents grounding, the foundation of life, substance, and connection to your Heart's Life Path. The Energy of the Open Heart - Connecting with heart space and remembering love.

As we begin, you'll get to know yourself through an exploration into the nature of being you, and an uncovering of who you want to BE. From here you'll grow grounded and rooted to the fullest expression of yourself, your Prosperous Path and your Wealth Creation wellspring.

WATER represents Emotional Release, Intuition, and Inner Reflection. The Energy of Healing Your Heart.

Next, you'll break down the barriers and uncover and clear what truly limits you. This process of uncovering, releasing, and deep clearing will allow you to grow and move forward with your own Inner Wealth of Knowledge — and then create from that unique space.

AIR represents intellect, intention, and Connection to Universal Life Source. The Energy of what is yet to be seen with the human eye, it's an inner Higher Wisdom. It is in constant movement and is barely noticeable to the human eye except when it is fierce and powerful. It is also refreshing and cleansing... think of blowing the cobwebs away to make room for what we are calling in.

Our exploration of AIR allows you to activate and connect with your Powerful Vision, setting and tuning in to it as your own personal compass bearing. You will have a clear inspired path guided by The Energy of your Envisioned future to creating your Elementally Abundant life for the greater good of all. Now the Magic begins!

FIRE represents the energy behind Inspired Prepared Action, a fuel for Transformation, representing Your Personal Power, and Inner Strength. It is the fire in your belly, the fire that moves us and fuels the action that must occur for anything to be created. And Abundant Creation requires bright, flaming Fires to Manifest.

It's time to ignite your Mission. You are a Creatrix and you are here to live with Impact, Joy, Ease and Prosperity. When you ignite the FIRE within you — the FIRE which supports Self-motivation — you will be inspired to take Aligned Action and transform Your life.

Is it time for you to BE who you were born to BE, and to be Elementally Abundant?

Will you let nature and the Cosmic Intelligence that runs through you — that IS you — be your guide?

The techniques and practices on these pages are borne of my experience as an intuitive coach, a spiritual mentor, and my training in positive psychology. We'll bridge the Mind, Body, and Soul connection for Elemental Success.

With that in mind, what does Success mean to you?

Consider it for a moment.

Is it about wealth, achieving certain accolades, being high up on the career ladder, the property ladder, or whatever other ladder we're supposed to be climbing?

Or it is something deeper?

For me, Success means having meaning and purpose in my Life. It's about a sense of connection — both to something bigger than me and to a sense of belonging and community. Success is about being in Flow and engaged in what I'm doing, experiencing positive emotions, meaningful relationships, and great health. And when I have all of that in balance my Prosperity flourishes.

As you read, you will notice I've used capital letters occasionally for some words, such as Love, Joy, Truth, Soul Purpose, and several others. I have chosen to do this any time I've sensed that emphasising a concept will make it more meaningful to you in that sentence, and in that moment. The intention is always to elevate the message in the hope it will connect with you on a deeper level.

AND NOW, I'M INVITING YOU TO MAKE YOUR OWN LEAP

Come with me as you get to know your True Abundant Self (EARTH), let go of anything and everything that limits you (WATER), align to your big Vision (AIR) and activate your personal Power and Inner Strength (FIRE).

Let's call on nature and the Cosmos.

Let's acknowledge and appreciate what a feckin' miracle you are... Not just a miracle, but MAGICAL AF.

This is where I can get a little impassioned... I think you can work out what AF stands for?!

Scientists say that the odds of you being born are one in a 400 trillion — and if that wasn't enough you're also made up of 97% stardust. The elements that were released in the big bang are the elements that make up your body... yeah, I'd say you're pretty miraculous!

So let's celebrate your awesomeness, move forward beyond your past limitations and towards your Fullest Magical Prosperous Potential.

You are the one your ancestors dreamed of. You are the One.

You are a magnificent badass Divine BEing and you are Powerful!

Let's surrender to the Magic and Light this world up together.

For together we Rise and Soar — as Heart Open and Free Soul Dancers.

My only ask of you right now is to read this book with a curious mind and a sense of adventure.

My only hope is that you will be moved to reclaim and own your Power, and use it to craft and cultivate your Highest, most Loving Elementally Abundant Life experience.

CHAPTER 3

How to Use This Book

"Success is a journey, not a destination. The doing is often more important than the outcome."

— Arthur Ashe

As you venture forward, I encourage journaling and note-taking.

There are exercises and prompts throughout this book based on positive psychology, ancient modalities, New Thought wisdom, mindset resets, and New Age practices that I have personally used with my clients and on my own journey to the ever-evolving fulfilment of my Vision and prosperous path. These will support you in your Soul growth, and strengthen personal connections with those in your life, too.

You'll also find reflections and suggestions throughout the unfolding of the journey, all to aid in deepening your growth and Soul work and to point you towards further readings when relevant.

I encourage you to observe your dreams, and if you like you can have a separate dream journal. Our unconscious loves to process our learnings and desires when we are in the expansive realm of dream time.

Notice any recurring messages or synchronicities in your waking and dream times.

Personally, I get a lot of my messages and best intuitive hits in the shower. Ah — you never know where inspiration will strike!

I see you all as Elemental Heart-led leaders, be you seekers, creatives, visionaries, healers, mothers, fathers, mystics, manifestors and Elemental changemakers.

Whether you know it or not yet, you are part of a tribe. Would you like to come and join your fellow Elementals in the free community I've created to accompany this book? I know that everything I'm sharing here has the power to change your life, and I also know that change gets even more powerful, and a lot more fun, when you share it with others.

Come and sit with us around the fire, share your insights, questions, musings and inspirations.

Come and be supported on your journey and discover ways you can go even deeper with the practices within this book.

You will find bonus material, PDF downloads, audio meditations, and videos from me to you, my dear creative elemental reader.

Come and join your Elemental community at www.ionarussell.com/elemental-circle.

And now, it's time for us to really begin. As you read and play with the possibilities in this book, I encourage you to have fun, and I invite you to smile with your Abundant Beautiful Heart.

CHAPTER 4

Preparing Yourself for the Journey

"Matter is energy. Energy is light. We are all light beings."
— *Albert Einstein*

It's time to loosen the valve and open the Heart Space.

Energy does not die. It cannot disappear, it can however become blocked and inhibit flow. We can also have slow energy, it can become sluggish, or in resistance, or out of step with us. The Life Energy source that exists is constant and present; energy is constant and always present. There are ways for us to loosen the valve and allow it to flow more freely — and that's what we'll do now to prepare ourselves for the voyage ahead.

Here's an empowering fact: you get to choose what your external energetic environment looks like and feels like AND you also have the power to cultivate your internal energetic connection to the Cosmic Life Source — and your Heart.

When we connect to our Hearts, and when we come from a space of calm, everything flows with so much more ease. That's our aim with the two practices I'm going to suggest you start with. They're a way to clear the decks and let go of unfinished business or any energetic ties that might be holding you back.

CLEARING YOUR EXTERNAL ENERGETIC ENVIRONMENT

Start by taking a moment to consider these questions:

How pleasing is your physical space to you?

Do you feel open and at ease in your physical space, or constricted and tense?

What about the space you work from? Is your desk tidy? Is there anything in your environment or on your computer that needs to be filed away, deleted, or completed?

What about your bedroom, is it peaceful and serene? Or do you have piles of clothes taking up space and adding to a sense of confusion and disarray?

If you're anything like me you might have a rather hefty 'junk drawer' — those spaces where we chuck anything miscellaneous, promising to sort it out later. And then... later never comes.

De-clutter any drawers, cupboards, or shelves you have like that today.

Clear away those piles of clothes, do your filing, and give your physical space a spruce up.

Do what you can do to clear physical space without getting overwhelmed. Really, what we've touched on here is the tip of the iceberg. There are entire books and courses dedicated to helping people clear clutter and create harmonious living and working environments. If you sense you need help in this area, follow your intuition and take any steps you need to. You don't have to de-clutter the entire house before continuing this book — let's be careful not to procrastinate!

Choose a few areas to clear and set the intention that you will continue to pay attention to creating a harmonious physical space as and when you can.

HEART SPACE ACTIVATION

It's time now to turn inwards. The very first place I like to start every day is from my Heart Space or the Heart energy centre. The Heart is the portal, the gateway to your Soul, your inner and outer rhythms, and of course, your Higher Self, your Authentic True Self. In this way, the Heart is almost our fifth Element, because it is so integral and essential to any expansion, growth or change we are inviting in.

I have two versions of the Heart Space Activation to share with you. The first is a quick Heart Space Activation, and then there's an additional up-level of the 4 Elements Heart Method which I have abbreviated to I♥4E. At this point on our journey, I don't want to overwhelm you with practices or 'things you must learn to do' before we go on, so this is a perfect opportunity for me to add the extended version of the Heart Space Activation to our free community group, here: www.ionarussell.com/elemental-circle

Throughout the book, you'll see I often invite you to drop into your Heart Space, and that might mean doing the shorter version I'm about to share here, or going deeper with the one in our community group. Do whatever feels right for you at the time. The added bonus of having the online space available to us is that I can share an audio recording of both versions, which are much easier to follow than written instructions on the page.

So let me start by sharing the printed version of the short and sweet Heart Activation process. You can read through and try it yourself, or you can open your phone or your laptop and download the audio from our community group.

Within this version, we'll also practice the HA breath, as taught by my Hawaiian guides. It is the Breath of Life and it is from the Heart. It takes us out of the analytical thinking mind, connects us to our Hearts, and opens the gateway to our Soul where all transformation happens.

HEART ACTIVATION
(Version 1)

Begin with eyes open or closed; I invite you to close them if you can.

Allow this moment to be a pause.

Now begin imagining your breath going in and out of your Heart.

Consciously breathe in through your nose and out through your mouth, while also keeping your awareness on your Heart. Keep picturing the breath going into and out of your Heart.

You can place a hand on your Heart if it helps you.

Notice how — so easily — you drop down from your head and into your Heart... This is where the magic happens.

Do this for three breaths or for five minutes or longer. Do what feels good for you.

Now, let's add in the HA breath.

This is my favourite go-to breath.

This is conscious and deliberate breathing.

Inhale through your nose . . .

Exhale through your mouth . . .

Inhale slowly and deeply, filling your stomach. Allow your stomach to relax.

Fill your torso and lungs, keeping your shoulders and jaw relaxed.

Exhale … making the "HA" sound on the exhale.

HA as in Alo-HA and HA-waii. It's like a big purposeful sigh.

Rest your hand on your chest, and feel the difference in your exhale as you make this sound, fully and completely emptying your lungs.

To me, this breath feels like a full mind, body, and Soul reset.

Do this three times or more.

You can do this anytime you desire or require it. As you read, you'll notice I suggest starting many of the exercises in the book with Heart Space Activation. It's a beautiful reset, a way to align.

If all you do for yourself daily is this, then you are already coming from an Elementally-aligned Soulful space with ease and Inner Peace. This is where creativity can be sparked rather than chaos.

HEART SPACE ACTIVATION
(Extended version 2)

In the extended version of this practice you will get to open your Heart even more by adding in the four key Elements to the process. You will be able to tune into your natural element to support you with where you are right now and what you are inviting into your life, all while honouring your own unique creating process. As mentioned above you will find this in your free community members' area at www.ionarussell.com/elemental-circle

Through this extended process you will bring all four elements into balance, fully integrating them to create your PURE Abundance from your Heart in all areas of your life. There is no other way to Pure Abundance unless you are in alignment with the four elements of

EARTH, WATER, AIR and FIRE.

I have one more offering for you before we move on. This next exercise is a favourite of mine, and it's one of the most beneficial and valuable practices you can gift yourself.

THREE GOOD THINGS EXERCISE

This is a gratitude exercise, also known as the Three Blessings Exercise. It has been shown to increase happiness and bring a deeper sense of well-being. It was created by Martin Seligman who is considered to be an expert on depression and happiness, and has been called the "Father of Positive Psychology."

I recommend you do this every day; I like to do it at night before going to sleep but if you find the morning is more spacious then do it then. As you begin, I invite you to first drop into your Heart Space with three deep breaths.

You are invited to think of three things that went well, and why, in the last 24 hours and write them down.

Reflect back on anything good that happened, anything that seems positive to you.

It is important to stick with ONLY three things.

Next, reflect on why each good thing went well. Determining the 'why' is the most important part of this exercise and takes it one step soulfully deeper than a basic gratitude practice.

Alternatively, you could spend time discussing this together with your partner, each sharing what has gone well for you today and why. Another approach that is particularly wonderful with children is to have a 'Three Good Things' jar which you all add to daily, then at the end of the week, or year, you can empty it out and read them.

And bonus points if you can focus on new unique good things each day. For best results do this for at least a week and keep in mind if do this for a year, avoiding repetition, you will have over 1,000 unique expressions of blessings in your life to celebrate. How expansive and joyful is this to know?

CHAPTER 5

Reflections & Suggestions: The Beginning of the Beginning

This is our first 'Reflections and Suggestions' chapter. These sections are invitations to pause, contemplate, and expand what you're discovering. Sometimes that happens with a simple acknowledgment and appreciation for where you are, other times you might feel inspired to follow a reference or do some investigative work of your own. The intention behind every point of reflection and each suggestion is to deepen the work you are doing with the four elements, to take you from feelings of lack and dissatisfaction to tuning into your prosperous Elementally Abundant Life.

1. Though we are at the start of our journey, I'd love you to please take a pause and honour yourself for the work you have done already. All journeys begin with a first step and you have very boldly taken yours. Well done.

2. Take some time to reflect on the exercises you've tried so far. Can you feel the spaciousness you are creating around you, in particular when you activate your Heart Space?

3. Doing the Heart Space Activation with the 4 Elemental Heart Method daily will increase your confidence, inner peace, and manifestation creation ability. Do this daily for four weeks and be amazed. If you miss a day, start again at day one. My clients have the most incredible breakthroughs and sense of Love for themselves and humanity. It just works.

4. The Three Good Things Exercise invites us to place our attention daily on what's good in our lives. I'm sure we all recognise the value in doing this, but I want you to notice the

real, tangible changes that this practice initiates when you do it regularly. Keep a note in your journal on how you feel and what you sense after doing it, and if you notice any changes occurring throughout the rest of the day, too.

5. For Further insight on the Three Good Things Exercise you can hear Martin Seligman discussing it here: https://sites.google.com/site/psychospiritualtools/Home/psychological-practices/three-good-things

PART 2: EARTH

The Foundations of Life

CHAPTER 6

The Earth Principle

EARTH represents grounding, the foundation of life, substance, and connection to your Heart's Life Path. The Energy of the Open Heart - Connecting with heart space and remembering love.

As we begin, you'll get to know yourself through an exploration into the nature of being you, and an uncovering of who you want to BE. From here you'll grow grounded and rooted to the fullest expression of yourself, your Prosperous Path and your Wealth Creation wellspring.

> *"The magic begins in you. Feel your own energy, and realize similar energy exists within the Earth, stones, plants, water, wind, fire, colours, and animals."*
>
> — *Scott Cunningham*

Now, our journey begins in earnest. It is time for you to get to know yourself. It's time to reconnect with nature and our beautiful, magnificent EARTH, and from that grounded place explore the nature of BEing you, by BEing present here and now, fully embodied as the magical BEing that you are.

With that in mind, The EARTH Principle is made up of two halves to echo that two-part process:

Step 1: Ground Thyself

Step 2: Know Thyself

This is the beginning of you discovering your Prosperous Path and your Elementally Abundant Life by drawing on the power of the elements, much like the ancient Polynesian way-finders who navigated by the stars and the winds. There was a deep knowing within them, and you too have your own deep Inner Knowing.

I believe we've lost sight of the way of the wizards, the witches, the Celts, the Kahuna, the truth seekers, the mystery makers, the spell weavers, the Merlins, and the magicians. We've lost our way, and we've become disconnected.

Disconnected from nature, ourselves, and the Divine.

And the Divine is in you. The Divine IS You.

You are the One, and you are part of this Universal Cosmic Dance. You are the one your grandmothers prayed for.

The element of EARTH brings us home to ourselves, our own Self Worth and Personal Power.

Whether being in nature is already part of the way you take care of yourself or whether this is new territory for you, I have some simple yet dynamic practices to share in the upcoming chapters.

Each activity connects us to the EARTH elements around us. As humans, we've lost touch with our connection to nature. We are nature so therefore we have lost touch with ourselves. It's time to reconnect.

It's time to ground ourselves, so we can get to know ourselves.

To prepare, let us begin by coming home to Mother Earth.

EARTHING EXERCISE

I invite you to start this first exercise outside. Whether that means heading out into your garden or walking to the nearest green space to your house — please do it. You will benefit so much from being outdoors.

Find a peaceful spot and begin by dropping into your Heart Space, as we did in Chapter 4: Preparing Yourself for the Journey. As I said back then, I recommend you always begin any practice from your Heart Space, either Version 1 or the full Elemental Heart Method, with conscious awareness, mindful breathing, and clear intention.

If you can go barefoot for this you will amplify your connection to the EARTH. That's what this exercise is about: a tapping in, a touching base, forging a connection with Mother Earth.

Your task is to simply walk, or stand in awareness, feeling the ground beneath you, supporting you.

After a moment or two, think of a tree rooted and grounded into the EARTH. How do you imagine this to feel, to be? Visualise roots spreading downwards from you and into the EARTH.

You can go deeper here by sitting or lying down, feeling Mother Earth's support beneath you. Let go of what no longer serves you. Let the EARTH transmute any worries, concerns, and troubles you may have. Breathe as you release them. Stay here as long as you like.

This is a favourite practice of mine. Sometimes when I go out into the garden I feel this deep need to lie on the ground and stay there a while. I always feel refreshed and replenished afterwards.

EARTH STEP 1:

Ground Thyself

CHAPTER 7

As Above, So Below

"Heaven is under our feet as well as over our heads."
— *Henry David Thoreau*

Just as a tree grows roots deep into the EARTH and is balanced by the equal reach of its branches, you too must become rooted as the fullest expression of yourself so you can reach the heights of the magic you are here to birth into this physical world. This is how you make the impact you came here to make, and the positive influence you were born to wield.

You are of the EARTH: a fact so many of us forget. As humans, we are mostly taught that the thinking mind is the aspect of us we should value above all else. As such we become overly head-led, trapped by analytical thinking, and a prisoner to worry and anxiety.

Some of us stay in that space, stagnating, while others break out and tread the inspired or spiritual path – a path I know you are treading too, by the very fact you are here. Only the danger then, for some, is that we become so enamoured by the realisation that we are more than our bodies that we try to escape them altogether, bypassing the fact that we are here as physical Beings. We become out of balance once again, and this time we float away, unmoored, uprooted, ungrounded, and disconnected.

To find the harmony and the equilibrium we must journey within. Acknowledging that we are of the EARTH, and tuning into all she is and all she can gift us, is crucial.

I have to ask when you think of the EARTH, what do you sense?

Do you feel the depth of her, the complexities, or is she simply a steady and grounded truth?

Do you perceive the EARTH as Mother Earth, here holding and nurturing you, sustaining you?

And do you Love her?

And ... do you Love yourself?

For you are one and the same. To Love Mother Earth is to Love yourself and the Divine magic that is within you. Yet our humanness can turn against us, and the stories we tell ourselves — namely that we are separate and disconnected from the Divine — impacts our view of life, as well as what we see as our place in the world.

We can doubt ourselves and our worthiness, find ourselves lacking when we compare ourselves to others, push ourselves and overwork as we strive for some level of predetermined financial success, and burn out as we force and push our way through the world. And, when we do step outside our comfort zone, that little nugget of imposter syndrome can sometimes be lurking around the corner.

We will explore all of this more deeply in the upcoming chapters.

For now, consider:

Who were you before they told you who you should be?

Now it is time to remember. It's time to cut the ties that have bound you, for you to once again be Abundantly Wild and Free. Yes, there is something paradoxical here; we're untethering what has kept you limited, while simultaneously rediscovering and planting the roots that allow you to be YOU in your truest, fullest, most magnificent form.

You will rise rooted and be magical.

The challenge within this element is in finding the balance: being Free while being Grounded. Nature is our way in.

BALANCING MEDITATION

This is a beautiful, tranquil meditation to ground you. Meditation without grounding leaves us unbalanced. So often seekers want to reach for the lofty heights of expansion, nirvana, or higher levels of consciousness by going up and forgetting to ground down as far, if not further. To be rooted in and of this life is to be balanced: as above, so below.

A tree without strong deep roots is easily uprooted and knocked off balance in turbulent times. A tree that is rigid and unwavering will snap and crack in the changing winds of time. The secret is to be a tree that is deeply rooted and can sway and move with the changing seasons and currents of change.

The following is a meditation influenced by Hugh Gilbert, in his book Free The Unicorn. You'll find an audio version of this meditation in our online group, so now might be the perfect time to visit there if you haven't already www.ionarussell.com/elemental-circle .

This meditation is best done standing, and please note there is no right way to do this and there is no wrong way to do this. This is a practice.

Start with three deep Heart breaths, connecting to your Heart.

Use your magical imagination to make this feel real and know that you are safe and Loved.

Now picture yourself standing in your favourite place on Mother Earth, real or imagined, somewhere you've been or desire to be.

With every breath feel the connection to the sacred EARTH below your feet, be it sand, EARTH, rocks, or roots.

With each in-breath feel the sacred EARTH begin to fill your feet, then feel it rise up through your legs, going further with each in breath. A little like the motion of sucking up slowly through a straw.

Smell that EARTH, feel the texture of it gradually filling you, unconditionally and safely, and lovingly.

When you fill completely, wait for a moment or two.

Then imagine a ball of gold or silver liquid or light above your head, which then floats down and fills you through from the top of your head all the way down your body. Allow the light or liquid to flow through you, and slowly with each exhale, feel that light or liquid begin to wash the Earth back down, taking with it anything that does not best serve you in that moment.

Feel that liquid rinsing out all the main tracts and nooks and crannies within you with each exhalation, until your whole body is clear.

Then, with each out-breath, continue to let the liquid or light flow down into the Earth gradually forming a root system. Some roots may go deep, others spread out close to the surface.

It's all good and it's all perfect.

When you feel your roots are firmly connected to the Earth, take a couple of slow deep breaths through your Heart, and then when you are ready open your eyes.

CHAPTER 8

The Power of Being in Nature

"Many eyes go through the meadow, but few see the flowers in it."

— *Ralph Waldo Emerson*

Nature empowers you; it nourishes your Soul and it's food for your wellbeing. My journey home to me began with many walks in nature, all the while being in the space of true gratitude for everything I saw: intricate and abundant flowers, the magnificence of a spider's web, morning dew drops, sun dancing through the trees, birds soaring on high. I vividly remember the first walk where I truly felt connected: I took a photo of a plant unfurling, just as I was unfurling and opening up to the magic that surrounded me.

Spending time out in the open is a key part of working with the element of EARTH. Even if you don't consider yourself an 'outdoors' kind of person, I am sure you've felt that beautiful unburdening that occurs in nature. And science backs this up: there is a growing body of research which supports the deep Truth that being in nature nourishes us and relieves stress, thus leading to feelings of happiness. It's more challenging to be creative and tap into our Soul Purpose if we are stressed and burnt out. Think of being in nature as a way to fill your creative soulful cup up.

PEACEFUL WALKING PRACTICE

Again, begin this practice by dropping into your Heart Space. If you wish, you can use this to extend the initial Earthing exercise we did as preparation for exploring the EARTH Principle, or you can do it separately.

This practice invites you to go on a walk and be fully present and in gratitude for all that you see and experience. Breathe deeply and calmly and allow yourself to be in the moment.

If the weather isn't suitable, you can still take a walk in nature without leaving the house... in your imagination.

Incredibly, our minds do not know the difference between what is real and what is imagined.

You may have heard of one of Dr. David R Hamilton's favourite scientific study on the power of our imagination, known as the Piano Study, which he references in his book *Why Woo-woo Works*. Two groups of volunteers practiced playing notes on a piano for two hours a day – only one group did this for real on a piano while the other group imagined they were playing the notes on a piano. Every day, each volunteer had a brain scan, and after the experiment, the results showed that the areas of the brain that were activated were identical in both the real and imagined group.

Isn't that amazing? The magic of your imagination is what sparks your creativity, your curiosity, and your intuition. Use it to create your walk, drawing on all five senses, and really let that beautiful imagination you have lead you.

Whether you take a walk for real or in your mind, be there — consciously. I had a client who took daily walks and was insistent that she enjoyed them. She could tell me where she'd been, and some of what she'd seen, but as we explored how she felt on the walk she realised she saw it as a thing to get done, and she was almost marching with her head down, just to tick it off her list and get back to work. So yes, she was getting exercise, and yes she was getting fresh air – but she wasn't present in her body or the experience.

The magic of a walk in nature when we are fully present is that it refuels us and allows creative ideas to drop in. So, on your walk, be in nature. Don't follow distracting thoughts. Don't rush. This isn't something to tick off or get done. Slow down, 'pop a squat' as they said in *Pretty Woman* — and be present.

CHAPTER 9

Learning to Fly

"When we become fixed in our perceptions, we lose our ability to fly."

— Yongey Mingyur Rinpoche

Just like the client I described a moment ago, I've also found myself out on a walk in nature with my head down, dogs running up ahead, and me marching on just to get the job done. When I return home from that kind of distracted walk, I feel stressed and irritated. I quickly realise I've limited my focus and haven't been present to myself, the walk, my surroundings, or the beauty that I have inevitably missed.

Our focus is a powerful thing. What you focus on can limit you and keep you stuck within a small box of misinterpretation and deception. Think of sitting on the edge of the Grand Canyon and having your view limited so that you miss the vastness and openness of what is all around you, and thus miss out on what is beyond your view.

When we open our view, both our internal and external perception, we increase our opportunities to fly beyond the walls of limitations. We open ourselves up to the infinite possibilities.

HAKALAU

The ancient Hawaiian practice of Hakalau expands our awareness in the present moment, and we can add it to any of the practices introduced so far.

Hakalau is believed to improve your concentration, the use of your senses, your ability to learn, and your overall performance. There are no distractions of negative emotions — only awareness in the present moment.

As Hugh Gilbert observes in his book Free the Unicorn, in Hawaii Hakalau has been successfully introduced into schools as a practical exercise to widen children's focus, and the results have been very powerful.

You can do this practice out in nature or while sitting comfortably at home.

Begin by gazing out in front of you.

Gently soften your focus; it can help to look at a spot on the wall or in the distance.

Become aware of your peripheral Vision.

Raise your hands directly in front of your face, in the 'thumbs up' position. Look at your thumbs.

Keeping your gaze forward, move your arms out in front of you, then slowly move them away from each other as far as you can — until your thumbs are just on the edge of your peripheral Vision. You can then drop your hands to your sides or keep them up.

Hold your softened gaze forward.

That's it — it's that simple. The key is in repeating it.

When I do this while out on a walk, I have a different awareness of my surroundings, and in particular, I become more conscious of the sounds happening around me. I also get some amazing ideas that I usually have to record into my phone so as not to lose them!

Just a note: if you choose to do this exercise while walking, please be careful.

If you do this practice regularly, you'll find over time that your peripheral Vision increases; I've seen this happen for many of my clients as their internal and external perception expands with a sense of spaciousness.

This practice is amazing for making space for creative ideas, contemplation, and intuitive insight.

CHAPTER 10

Reflections & Suggestions: Ground Thyself

1. The Earthing exercise and the Peaceful Walk Practice are both underpinned by a sense of presence and BEing in the moment. When you are deliberately grounded in nature or walking peacefully, how do you feel? How easy is it to pay attention and be in the moment?

2. When you get back home after trying these practices, notice how the rest of the day plays out for you. Is it possible to take that sense of connectedness with you into the rest of the day?

3. When you tried the Hakalau Practice, did you become aware of your other senses improving? Perhaps you noticed a sense of expansion or spaciousness. And what about your levels of creativity and inspiration? After practicing this for several days, notice if you have more of those magical ah-ha moments.

4. Gratitude has the power to enhance and expand any experience. What if, next time you're in nature, you tap into the energy of gratitude? What does it bring to the experience?

5. Nature is a great restorer and invigorator. Keep a note in your journal on how you feel as you tap into this energy and space more and more. Notice any changes you observe and always stay curious.

6. In the coming days and weeks, pay particular attention to any insights, ideas, or inspired actions that appear to drop into your awareness in unexpected ways.

7. There is an area of science referred to as eco-psychology

which includes activities such as nature therapy, wilderness therapy, forest bathing, ecotherapy and so on. Practitioners and facilitators say that our physical and mental well-being are enhanced when we spend time out in nature. There's a reduction in anxiety, improvements in our stress levels and attention to detail, and an increase in creativity and our ability to connect with other people. Nature therapy pillars are based on the five senses of sight, sound, smell, touch, and taste. You can find out more in the following articles: https://www.verywellmind.com/how-nature-therapy-helps-your-mental-health-5210448 https://www.ncbi.nlm.nih.gov/pmc/articles/PMC4997467/ https://www.ncbi.nlm.nih.gov/pmc/articles/PMC5663019/

8. In Chapter 8 I shared from Dr.David Hamilton's book *Why Woo-woo Works* published by Hay House (2021). He's also written many other amazing books. I highly recommend you check him out.

9. I have mentioned Hugh Gilbert's book a couple of times already. He was a great mentor of mine and has since transitioned. His book *Free The Unicorn* is available online and is published by Larry Czerwonka Company. He is mentioned again further in this book.

EARTH STEP 2:

Know Thyself

CHAPTER 11

Living With Joy, Love, and Gratitude

"Know that joy is rarer, more difficult, and more beautiful than sadness. Once you make this all-important discovery, you must embrace joy as a moral obligation."

— *André Gide*

So many seekers begin their journey by looking outside of themselves for a leader, a mystic, a guide – essentially, someone 'who knows more' than them.

I am not that person.

This is a book, and a process, whereby you get to know yourself, unearth what Elemental Abundance is for you and how you are going to create with ease and impact. That's our over-arching aim, and it's the particular aim of the following set of chapters, as we move from digging into the EARTH in Step One, to now growing from the EARTH in Step Two.

To know thyself happens only when you Love yourself, as you are, and each and every aspect of your Heart and Soul: your magnificent Cosmic stardust particles, and your perfectly imperfect humanness.

It is when you see yourself as unconditionally worthy of Love that the real breakthroughs come. You no longer look to external gratification, external validation, or external approval. You no longer try to fill the void left by wounds made in this lifetime or others. You understand you are not an empty vessel needing to be filled. You let the walls you have built around yourself, your Heart, and your Truths — dissolve. You let the light in.

And you do this from a place of truly honouring yourself, seeing yourself, and BEing yourself. It's not so much about the DOing, it's about BEing. That's how our Elementally Abundant Life unfolds before and around us, and how we go from dissatisfaction and feelings of lack to a place of fully-embodied Heart opening, Self Love, Self Worth and knowing our true value.

Loving yourself is all that is necessary. As the great Marianne Williamson says, "There is only love, and fear is a call to love."

LET GO OF JUDGEMENT AND RESISTANCE

Choose to let go of judgement, for yourself and others. When we judge we only attract more of whatever we're judging into our experience. Forgiveness and Compassion are the keys to Self-Love.

That doesn't mean judgments won't come up, we're human after all. So always be gentle with yourself.

Be gentle for you have chosen to step into this magnificent feckin' Universe and be human here now. For some of us, it's more challenging than it is for others. Some of us resist the Love. Some of us resist the kinship, the clarity, the belonging, the community, but it doesn't need to be so complicated.

We can make it simpler, and the exercises and practices I'm about to share to help you Love and connect with yourself will do just that. It all begins and ends with your Heart.

When we live and breathe from our Heart, we choose Love over Fear. In choosing from Love, we choose what's in alignment for ourselves and the Greater Good, and we choose with compassion and a deeply felt sense of being connected to everything. But when we choose from fear, we choose from a sense of being separate and stuck in our mind. I heard Robert Holden call the state of being stuck in our heads and overthinking as living from "the penthouse of our bodies vs living from our Heart". When we drop down into our Heart we choose Love, and to live from a loving space where we can do no harm.

And from there, perhaps you'll find that deeper meaning, that sense of accomplishment and engagement you experience when you're in flow as the dear and beautiful Soul that you are. You'll nurture and Love yourself, the EARTH, your surroundings, your business, your life, you, and who you choose to be.

And ...

WHO YOU CHOOSE TO BE IS TOTALLY UP TO YOU

It's time to stop doing the things that don't light you up. It's time to let go of the things you don't have to do; let go of the things that get in your way.

You are here to flourish both personally and for the greater good, creating your own unique impact here, on, and for this planet.

The question I invite you to get curious about right now is:

What is it that's going to feed your Soul? What will make your Soul nourished from the inside out?

A more direct way of putting it might be:

What is it that brings you feckin' Joy? What brings you ecstatic connectedness and belonging, that has your Heart bursting with Joy and bliss? What makes you know you are part of something bigger?

You don't need to have the answers right now, just a willingness to explore and uncover what is here for you.

And please keep in mind, when it comes to joy, that it's not always about having a blissful, heightened, explosive, pleasurable experience — because pleasure isn't necessarily relaxing and grounding. Sometimes it's intense and elevating. In the midst of vibrant ecstasy, you can have an out-of-body experience... That's amazing but not what we're going for just yet!

This is about connecting to the EARTH, to your world, to the ground. And joy can be peaceful. Joy can be grounding.

Think of the roots of the tree going down into the EARTH; think of the serenity you feel by the ocean or in the mountains or in a forest. That peacefulness, that joy, can spring from the simplest of things, not only in nature but elsewhere too. It might be in hearing a child laugh, helping a client reach their fullest potential, writing a book, or baking the best cookies in the entire world.

So your question is: What is it that brings you Joy — in a peaceful, grounded way? Because this is about connecting to the EARTH. This is about being rooted in the essence of who you are.

It is time for you to venture forth and begin to fully embody the wisdom of your insights and learning on this journey as it unfolds. To flourish you need to integrate all you discover into your Essence, and become the Truth of who you are through lived experience, processes, and exercises.

JOY JIGSAW

This is one of my favourite exercises to spark Joy. You get to explore what brings you Joy and to get curious about adding more of it into your life.

Grab a piece of paper and divide it in half, lengthways. On one side write down anything and everything that you can remember that has ever brought you Joy, made you feel happy or carefree, or inspired you. A clue is sometimes in the silliness; as adults, we tend to shy away from being silly. There are no rules to this except to have fun with it.

On the other side make a list of the things you're curious about trying, doing, or experiencing. Some of these might be simple like salsa dancing or learning to knit, or a bit more epic such as a holiday in the Seychelles or trekking through the Himalayas.

Then, each day, do something from one of your lists. Now, I get that some of the smaller Joys might be easier such as dancing in the rain, and others like traveling to the rainforest will take some major planning. But you can still begin to explore those bigger Joys, perhaps by starting a Vision board or Pinterest board with inspiring images, or by watching a documentary and getting a sense of the place or the topic.

What is great about the Joy Jigsaw is that it's dynamic and flexible – you get to add to your lists and delete things that just don't float your boat anymore. Perhaps as a teenager, you remember loving skiing but now you just can't stand the cold. If you try something and no longer enjoy it then take it off your list. Remember to celebrate yourself and have a laugh about it! The secret is to keep on being curious and keep trying things from your lists every day. You might just find a hidden talent.

The Joy Jigsaw is a great exercise to do with your family, partner, or children. You might also like to have a Joy Jar, rather than a list, and you can pick out a new piece of paper each day. Remember to keep adding to your Joy Jars.

Professor Barbara Fredrickson's work on positive emotions has found that "Positivity transforms us for the better" and increases our ability face challenges and adversity. In her book *Positivity* she wrote, "By opening our hearts and minds, positive emotions allow us to discover and build new skills, new ties, new knowledge, and new ways of being."

Enjoy creating your Joy Jigsaw and relish bringing in more positive emotions into your life. Think of the process as a way to nurture and grow your innate magnificent superpowers.

CHAPTER 12

Embodied Emotional Health

"True power is living the realization that you are your own healer, hero, and leader."

— *Yung Pueblo*

We all have innate well-being, health, and happiness within us; you came into this world divinely beautiful and magical. As we grow from the EARTH, let us restore the balance and align with your natural state of Being, of innate emotional health.

Let me first ask you, how are you treating your physical body?

We all know we need to eat nutritious food, drink water, move and sleep. Yet so many of us aren't or haven't been respectful of our own bodies.

I have personally been very unkind to my own body over the years, starting at age fourteen as a failed anorexic and then thinking I found the Holy Grail with bulimia. In my darkest days, I attempted suicide, and at various stages of my life I've given in to excessive consumption of alcohol and drugs. This is not a guided walk through the halls of my demons, but I wanted to share that we all have had our battles.

All those behaviours were ways of seeking external validation and forms of self-punishment. If you are struggling with any of these issues there are so many great organisations out there to support you, and I encourage you to seek the help and guidance you need.

What has helped support my own healing journey is a return home to 'Self' with Love and the realisation that everything I was seeking was here all along, inside my own Heart. It has been the inner work that I am sharing in this book and in my other works that have empowered me to claim my sovereignty. The greatest gift along the journey came in nurturing nourishing positive friendships that have supported my growth, along with developing a transcendental meditation practice and energy work.

WHAT FEEDS YOUR MIND AND SOUL?

I'd like you to consider not only what you're giving your body to consume, but also what you're giving to your mind. What books are you reading? Whose podcasts are you listening to? How much time are you spending down the rabbit hole of social media? Who are you spending your time with, and are they a positive influence, encouraging you and inspiring you?

Think of all this as energy that you are feeding your Soul Self to grow, flourish and prosper.

You have the choice to choose the energy that you feed your Soul with, and I invite you to choose wisely.

EMOTIONAL AWARENESS

Becoming aware of our emotions is the first step to understanding and reflecting on our emotional health, and in doing so we can also learn to raise our vibration. Now, when people talk about 'raising your vibe', what are they referring to exactly? I find the emotional vibrational energy spiral image really useful here.

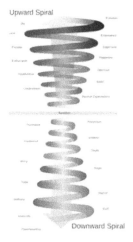

On the ascending spiral, you'll see we have positive emotions, ascending up through Contentment, Happiness, Empowerment, Love, Joy, Peace, Freedom. On the flip side, the descending spiral starts at boredom and spirals down to frustration, impatience, worry, anger, fear.

So to 'raise our vibe' is to move up through the spiral. I'd suggest moving up one step at a time, so you don't get caught in fake or toxic positivity. I'm not of the 'fake it til you make it' crowd. You have to feel into the way you want to be and how you want to live, and the feeling has to be authentic and real for you. Our subconscious believes everything we tell it, and if we venture into the realm of the unbelievable our own personal negative gremlins can step onto our shoulders and call us out. And then we're descending down the spiral as a gremlin says, *No, you won't / can't / shouldn't. Who do you think you are to do X, Y, Z...?*

I invite you to explore and discover for yourself what the experiences are that bring positive feelings to you, and how you can consciously include these in your daily life. Looking for the mini miracles, being curious, finding the pockets of Joy, and practicing daily gratitude will all improve your emotional state.

Positive Psychologist Barbara Fredrickson calls this "the upward spiral of positive emotion" and found that we need three positive experiences to counteract one negative. "When people experience positive emotions, their minds broaden and they open up to new possibilities and ideas. At the same time, positive emotions help people build their personal well-being resources, ranging from physical resources to intellectual resources, and social resources."

Before we move on to my biggest love in this area of restoration and mindfulness, let us take a second to discuss your gut. Not your gut *instincts* — we'll be diving into the magical mysteries of those in the next section, but your physical gut, the one which houses 80% of your immune system. Does that fact surprise you…? It did me.

Essentially it means a healthy gut is a healthy you. To top it all off 90% of the happy hormone serotonin lives there too, so if you're not nourishing your gut and caring for it with good stuff this can lead to fewer happy hormones and increased feelings of sadness, depression, and low mood. This brings a whole new perspective to the phrase, "You are what you eat."

A healthy body supports a healthy mind, diminishes stress, and increases our ability to be resilient, optimistic, creative, and inspired, helping us to thrive in all areas of our lives.

So always keep this question on your radar: *What am I feeding my body, mind, and Soul today?*

Now it's time to talk more about the really good bit (cue chilled music) of restorative practises and mindfulness. Ahhh… Om… Meditation.

MEDITATION

When I was at my lowest, meditation saved me. It called me home to my Authentic Soulful Self. It didn't bring some ecstatic 'Hallelujah' moment, it was more subtle than that. It was a Peaceful and Heart-grounding experience. Of course, what works for me may not work for you. The aim is to find a form of being with yourself, quieting your mind, and just BEing present.

Meditation doesn't need to be you sitting in a cave or on top of a hill. Do something that fits into your day. When are you most mindful and present?

For some of you, meditation might look like resting on a park bench listening to the birds or sitting on your meditation cushion for ten or twenty minutes. Others might get lost in the 'Zen zone' while painting or drawing, creating sand mandalas, or walking in nature and BEing in expanded awareness. (Refer back to Hakalu in Chapter 9, and don't forget the Earthing/grounding practices in Chapter 6.)

Whatever it is for you do more of that and BE Fully Present!

Meditation improves our creativity and self-reflection skills. It helps maintain mental resilience, lowers stress, and improves our memory and cognition. My clients and I have found that it improves our overall mood, helps us to bounce back quicker from knockbacks, and makes us less shouty. That's a technical term. Seriously, I was a really shouty parent before I started meditating – just ask my son. It's not how we behave on the meditation cushion it's how we show up in real life. With practice meditation and the Zen state can become your natural state.

One thing is certain, throughout the day we have around 80,000 thoughts (I don't know how they counted them, but they did the research in Maryland university) and one of the biggest barriers people have to trying meditation is that they think they have to stop those thoughts in order to do it 'right'. Well, I'm not that enlightened. What we can do is get better at not holding onto the thoughts as they pop into our minds during meditation.

There are a couple of ways to do this.

Start by sitting up nice and tall or simply lay flat with your eyes closed, whatever is comfortable for you. Then, whenever a thought pops in, just let it be … and then let it float off.

One thing we know for sure is that another thought will be along soon ... and that's okay.

Don't fight thoughts, and don't be frustrated that they are there. Don't tell yourself not to have a thought (it's like telling yourself to not think about pink elephants), but also don't interact with the thought.

What do I mean by not interacting with it? Let's say you think, I forgot to buy milk. That might be true, but then you may start thinking, *Who forgets to buy milk? Why didn't I just remember I need to buy milk? I'll get it on the way home...* That's interacting with the thought! Just let it go.

Meditating for five to ten minutes a day will help calm and relax you. You can either breathe normally, or you can try breathing in through your nose and out through your mouth in a nice, smooth, natural rhythm. You might choose to rest your focus on that rhythm, though my favourite place to focus on is the Heart, not just in meditation but in all that I do. I may have mentioned this already!

There is another area of mindfulness called the 'art of contemplation', a term used in the title of Richard Rudd's book. As Rudd notes, contemplation is a proactive way in which mindfulness and intentional thought "engages the power of the mind, emotion, and body".

This is not to say that you think of a question or theoretical thought and work hard to focus on it until you get an *ah-ha* moment. It's about putting forth a question and letting it go and waiting for the Divine spark of the *ah-ha* to drop into your awareness.

As Rudd points out, most of us will have experienced contemplation when we are pondering something and then the solution, creative idea, resolution, or moment of clarity and insight appears to drop in, as if emerging from some wise place within us.

I don't know about you but as I mentioned before, I get all my best *ah-ha* moments in the shower! And sometimes I get them when I'm out walking, as long as I'm following my own advice from Chapter 8 and partaking in a Peaceful Walking Practice. My conscious monkey mind is occupied and therefore not overanalysing, and just by BEing in the present moment, suddenly inspiration strikes, and those *ah-ha* moments appear.

Where do you find you get those magical ideas? This is your invitation to consider consciously creating more moments like this. Less trying; more BEing present.

STEPS TO EMBODIED HEALTH

In this chapter I've shared a lot of information on the health of the mind, body, and Soul, it's up to you how you would like to move forward and start integrating these practices into your own life. The main thing I would like you to take away is that there are a multitude of ways to nourish our body, to feed your Soul, and to restore the balance within. Have fun, be curious and keep an open mind as you explore what works for you. One person's boredom is another person's tranquillity.

Here are eight inspired steps to improve your well-being and emotional health for your best self.

1. Nourish your body with whole foods that are full of nutrients. You can find tons of information on this online.

2. Eat mindfully. Pause before eating, be grateful, and consciously eat your food, savouring it.

3. Move your body for the love of it. No more thinking, I *have to* do this. Find movements and exercise that you love, that ground you, strengthen you. It's up to you. Just find something that brings you Joy.

4. Choose what you read and listen to. This is food for your mind.

5. Meditate to levitate your inner world. Remember this is about you finding a form of meditation that nourishes you. This may

be sitting quietly, listening to guided visualisations, painting, drawing, or doing a walking meditation. It's totally up to you what feels right – because there is no way to do it wrong. It's all a personal practice.

6. As I mentioned earlier, just doing the Ha breath and the Elemental Heart Activations will improve your wellbeing too. I advise my clients to do these daily.

7. Practise the art of contemplation.

8. Include restorative practices in your daily life. Make a list of what you find restorative. e.g. breathwork, shake it off and dance, an afternoon siesta, singing, reading, walking. It's your list. There are no rules.

CHAPTER 13

Intuition

"At any moment you truly have a choice that will either lead you closer to your spirit, your innate wisdom, your intuition. . . or further away from it."

— *Thich Nhat Han*

Your intuition is your superpower.

This is one of my favourite topics and it's also one that so many people are curious about. Learning how to tap into our intuition and use it to guide our choices is a complete game-changer.

Let's start with some magical super-powerful numbers. In the previous chapter, we learned that the gut houses 80% of our immune system and produces 90% of our serotonin. Now buckle up for one more super-epic gut fact: Your gut has 100 million neurons – that's 31 million more than your spinal column. WOW.

On top of that, it's often referred to as 'the belly brain' because it uses sensations to communicate with you. I'm certain you've experienced this! You might feel sick when you know you're making a tough decision, or if you're in a situation you'd rather not be in, your body will really let you know about it.

So yes – your gut communicates with you, and it does it faster than Deadpool speeding through the air on a unicorn at 100th of a millisecond. Understanding your gut feelings, your gut instinct – *your intuition* – is a bigger superpower than Beyoncé and Elton combined.

Some believe their intuition is a connection to their Inner Knowing, others attribute it to a Higher Self, or a Higher Consciousness, or to the Divine, or to angels. Whatever it is for you, that's what it is, and you can choose to tune into it.

The definition of intuition, according to the Oxford English Dictionary, is "the ability to understand something instinctively, without the need for conscious reasoning." It's a very personal and intimate capacity, in fact, think of it as 'in-to-me-I-see'.

Following your intuition means making decisions through 'feeling it' and knowing what to do without analytical thought. It's something that science has had trouble quantifying. The basic truth of the matter is everyone has intuition, and through practice, we can all access it and use it to guide our everyday lives.

Is it time to tune into this Superpower, your Inner Knowing, your Inner Wisdom — and listen to the whispers of your Soul, already waiting to inspire you?

RECOGNISING YOUR INTUITION

Centuries ago, we moved through our whole lives guided by intuition; it's how our ancestors lived, before analytical thought and brain-based thinking took over. Your intuition is part of your humanness. You had it as a child, we all did.

Children live life from a space of deep inner guidance: they play, run, laugh, eat, sleep and express themselves in a very authentic way, moment by moment. They're excellent at picking up on feelings, vibes, energies. But as they get older, they begin to override their natural knowing in order to fit into family life, peer groups, the education system, and other structures and institutions that prize logic and intellect. The more they listen to external input, the less Trust they have for their own Inner Self.

That's what happened to you; it happened to all of us.

But the beautiful thing is we can re-awaken our intuition, and learn to make decisions from that space of Inner Knowing. The more we practice using our intuition the stronger it becomes.

EVERYTHING YOU SEEK IS WITHIN YOU

Have you ever walked into a room and just got a 'feeling' about something, somebody, or the place in general? Where you just know instantly whether the vibe in the room is friendly or unfriendly, or if there's somebody who is particularly shy over in a corner, or if there are people arguing, or even just tension between certain people. Often, you can't actually see or hear any of these things with your usual five senses, but you know there's something there all the same.

That's your gut instinct. Your intuition.

Another way to recognise and acknowledge your intuition is to think of a time when you ignored it. Maybe you made a certain decision, perhaps to go somewhere, or say something, or take a job, or marry someone ... and after the fact, you were like, *Feck, I know I shouldn't have done that!*

It's weird how often we can know something intuitively and yet still ignore it. The key is not only learning to listen to our intuition but also to trust it.

Personally, I've had some amazing flashes of insight from my intuition in totally unexpected ways. Here's an example. I was on holiday with my family in Italy and we were catching the train to Florence (keep in mind I don't speak a word of Italian). The train was jam-packed and I suddenly sat up straight and said, "I have a funny feeling we are on the wrong train." I hadn't even thought about it, I just blurted it out. We were indeed on the wrong train and promptly disembarked just in time to catch the right train going in the right direction!

For the rest of that holiday, everyone would ask, "Do you have any funny feelings, Iona?" All said in jest and with love. This was a small example of trusting my intuition – big or small, it's all the same.

LETTING YOUR INTUITION GUIDE YOU

So how can we know when we're living via our intuition, and when we're overriding it?

It's actually pretty straightforward. When we ignore and override our intuition, we find life harder, more of a hassle, heavier. But when we're tapped into it, we sense we're in the flow, in the zone, and everything feels light and feels easy.

We get more right-place-right-time moments. More access to inspiration. We have more energy. We might still face struggles, because life sometimes sucks, but we now have access to this incredible superpower to guide us out of those difficult times.

When your intuition is telling you not to do something, you might feel an ache, a flattening, or just a sense of restriction. Any time I've ignored my intuition I've sensed it very clearly in my body, either by feeling sick to my stomach or by getting physically tired and overwhelmed, which can sometimes lead to an ear infection. In short, I feel it physiologically when I choose to tune my Inner Knowing out.

At the other end of the scale, when something is right for you, you might feel open and expansive. There's spaciousness and ease in your body, rather than tightness or dread.

As we learn to trust that intuition, to follow it and not override it, the messages become clearer and easier to translate.

We also feel more supported and Self Empowered – even when we're in those difficult situations or when we feel like we're struggling, because we access a level of inner peace as we follow our own navigation system.

To sum up:

- *Paying attention to what's going on around you is key.*

- *Notice what you're picking up on.*

- *See how you think about it and how you feel.*

BECOMING A MASTER OF INTUITION

The more you practice, the more you'll intuitively realise things that you may not have picked up on before. Pay attention not just to your internal world, but also your external world, and notice how you are reacting in it and what you're observing. It's like learning how to tune your radio, your antennae, to pick up on the vibes.

A key component of mastering your intuition is being willing to be present and in the moment with it. Put your phone down, sit peacefully, and observe. Keep returning to the present moment and keep tuning your radio.

The really amazing thing about your intuition is you can use it for pretty much anything. From big decisions to the small. Just stop, pay attention, and ask yourself whatever question you'd like guidance on. You may be surprised with the answer. As you learn to trust your Inner Knowing, using it practically like this becomes the norm.

'Practical' is a good word to introduce here, although perhaps it's not one you expect to hear in a chapter on intuition. But there's something to be said for blending your intuition with rationality because there will be times when your intuition guides you to do something that you might not be able to do in the real world, or to a situation out of your control. This is when common sense comes in, and the willingness to step back and look at the bigger picture.

For example, if you work for someone else, there may be times or occasions where you know intuitively that there are easier or more progressive ways of running the business. But when those decisions are out of your control, or when you sense that your suggestions won't be received well, you need to get practical. This is when you zoom out and sense the bigger picture. Sure, it can feel icky when we have to do something that is out of alignment with our Inner

Knowing, but it happens when we live and work with other people. Sometimes we just have to learn to energetically rise above the situation and work to the best of our ability with no malice or bad intentions. If you find yourself in this position, you can settle into your Heart space and imagine sprinkling love on to the situation and then you can just move on.

Essentially, learning to listen to your intuition is like learning to follow your own internal guidance system, your own natural GPS. It's your journey to navigating life from your own Inner Power.

This is how we tune into and live in our Dharma, the ancient Sanskrit word that loosely means to live your Soul's Purpose or righteous living. It's important to note that living your Dharma is not just about what you do, but how you do it, and why you do it, and to do it in *your own unique expression of yourself.*

> *"It is better to live your own Dharma imperfectly than to live an imitation of somebody else's life with perfection."*
>
> — *Bhagavad Gita*

To live inspired with our intuition is to live in elemental alignment with our Authentic True Self.

DIVINATION METHODS TO SUPPORT INTUITION WORK

I can't talk about intuition and not mention divination methods such as oracle cards, tarot cards, runes, tea leaves, pendulums, communicating with guides and so many other modalities. These are all great tools to connect with your intuition, and you also don't have to use any of them. In honesty, they are nice to have, and they can act as a gateway, but they're not essential. Says I with a drawer full of a gazillion decks! I can't help it, there's always one more deck I just get drawn to. I let the pictures do the talking.

My mum gifted me my first deck of tarot cards when I was fourteen, they were her old Rider Waite deck. I was curious about their messages and used to feel into the images from my Heart Space and listen to what they communicated to me. And now here I am working on creating my own intuitively guided cards. They are still in the 'musing' stage.

I invite you to investigate, use and play with any divination methods that call to you.

STEPS YOU CAN TAKE RIGHT NOW TO TUNE INTO YOUR INTUITION

Learning to trust and tune into this superpower might be easier than you think. It's essentially about remembering who you are as a magical magnificent BEing, and recognising that all that you seek is within you.

1. The easiest way to do this is to just find a moment where you can be quiet and calm. You don't have to be in total quiet, or on a mountain top. This is the real world! Intuition is about your interpretation of the insights and messages you get.

2. If you have a question you want to ask write it down, speak it out loud, visualise or ask it in your head (whatever works and feels comfortable) and then sit quietly or consider the art of contemplation as mentioned in the previous chapter.

3. Meditation can be a great way to clear the channel between you and your Inner Knowing. When you come out of meditation ask yourself the question from step 2 again, and you might find you just know the answer.

4. Pay attention to repeated messages in songs and any images or symbols you see often. Keep a note of what they come to

represent for you. For example, when I see butterflies I know it's my mum confirming something to me. Or when I'm told a number of times by different sources to read a book or check out a recommended course, I pay attention. Or perhaps a location just keeps coming into your awareness? It's up to you to follow the breadcrumbs.

5. Reflect on a time when you know you ignored your intuition and notice how that felt in your body, feel the sensations of knowing ... and then ignoring them. Notice how different that feels to when you know something and act on it.

6. Free-write in your journal, allowing your intuition to write through you. Don't worry about sentence structure, spelling, or neatness, and let the first couple minutes be nonsense if need be.

7. Set an alarm for 11:11 every day and look back over the last 24 hours and notice any miracles, moments of gratitude, and intuitive hits you had. These are sometimes easier to see in hindsight, which is why pausing in this way to reflect is a great way to recognise them. Make a note of anything that comes up on your phone for ease, or in your journal if this is convenient. Drop into your HEART space as you do this. Consistency is key here, so make sure that you set that alarm and take the time to do it, no matter what else is going on. It only takes 60 seconds.

8. Keeping a dream journal is another great technique. I don't recommend buying a dream dictionary – even though I had one as a teen (didn't we all at some point?!) It's more precise if you start to recognise what symbols mean for you. For one person, dreaming of being in the ocean on a sailboat might mean adventure and freedom, but for another person who has a fear of water, it might be a triggering dream and represent something else entirely. Create your own meanings. Keeping a dream journal makes it easier to see messages or recurring themes.

9. Breathwork is another amazing way to tap into your unconscious and intuitive guidance. There are many methods and techniques out there, find a method, or methods, that feel aligned for you.

10. A quick search online for the vibrational energy scale will illustrate the concepts of the emotional spiral up and down. This scale is referred to a lot by those talking about manifestation. If you haven't yet heard of Abraham Hicks, you will find some fabulous talks on YouTube and books.

CHAPTER 14

Personal Values to Empower You

"That is the ultimate question for all of us: do our actions reflect our values? Do our traditions reflect our beliefs? Do our purchases reflect our ethics? After all, what's the point in having values if we don't manifest them in our behaviour?"

— Colleen Patrick-Goudreau

Aligning with the Truth of who you are sounds lovely in theory, doesn't it? But what about in practice? How willing are you to put the work in to really understand who you are, and how you can initiate the kind of change you were born to create?

I guess that might not be a question for you, because as you're still here, fourteen chapters in, I get the sense that you are willing. As long as you're practicing and trying out the tools, techniques, and concepts I'm sharing. And you are, right?!

If you're committed to doing the work, you might even be what my friend and publisher Sean Patrick of The Good House Publishing calls a 'new age dropout' (wish I'd thought of that first, it's freakin' good).

If you're disillusioned by the overly happy and hyper-positive – as in toxically positive – perspective of some areas of the spiritual and new age community, you might be a new age dropout. A major irritation for me, and many others, are the coaches or groups who claim to have 'the answers'. Remember no one has the feckin' answers for you – except you. And no amount of 'slapping a happy smile on it or meditating your woes away is going to make you happy. Honestly, I could write a book about the dangers of toxic positivity and spiritual bypassing, but there are plenty already out there. I'll channel my energy here, in a much more constructive way!

The crux of all of this is you have to do your own inner work with integrity, and the truth is there are both highs and lows on that journey. And navigating it is a heck of a lot easier if we can get clear on our values and our own view on life. This includes facing anything which we might be avoiding, something we'll dive deeper into in the next section.

Your values allow you to weather any storm – and enjoy the calm seas, too.

IDENTIFYING YOUR VALUES - AND WHERE THEY COME FROM

So, how do you know what your values are?

Consider what motivates you, and steers or guides you forward.

Also, think about what distracts you, trips you up or hinders you.

I'll share a secret: the things that stall you or hinder you are usually your indication that you are not living to your own personal values.

You might be surprised to learn that a lot of what we attribute to our personal value system is learned behaviour from our environment, our family, our peers, and the myriad of information we're subjected to every day from various directions.

We're not going to dive into the nature/nurture debate here, though there will be more on this when we explore the WATER element, but so often we are living our lives from other people's patterns, values, and expectations. Either that, or we're heading for burnout because we're trying to 'fix' what we aren't naturally good at, or we're striving for success based on society's expected values and results.

As a side note, the way society is structured is so focused on our weaknesses, what we aren't good at, and what we need to work on more to be a success – and quite frankly it's stifling and extremely disempowering. By bringing focus to what we are naturally good at empowers us and helps us thrive and flourish.

Reflecting on our values allows us to see what truly motivates us and how we can live from our strengths in the face of adversity. We can also bring awareness to what our roadblocks are. A great way to deal with this is to become the observer; my favourite thing to say when I uncover something that might be holding me back is, "Isn't that interesting?" And then I move on.

To get more clarity on what your values are, I invite you to consider the following three questions and then take a look at the list of values in the table below.

What do you value most in life?

What are the values that reflect a life well lived for you?

What are you willing to be a stand for?

Choose intuitively, and be open to letting yourself be guided. This list isn't exhaustive, you can add to it and create your own.

Accountability	Ethics	Knowledge
Achievement	Excellence	Leadership
Adaptability	Fairness	Learning
Adventure	Faith	Legacy
Altruism	Family	Leisure
Ambition	Financial	Love
Authenticity	Forgiveness	Loyalty
Balance	Free-spirited	Making a difference
Beauty	Freedom	Openness
Being the best	Friendship	Optimism
Belonging	Fulfilment	Order
Career	Fun	Parenting
Caring	Future	Patience
Collaboration	Generosity	Peace
Commitment	Giving back	Power
Communication	Grace	Pride
Community	Gratitude	Recognition
Compassion	Growth	Resourcefulness
Competence	Harmony	Respect
Confidence	Health	Responsibility
Connection	Home	Risk-taking
Contentment	Honesty	Safety
Contribution	Hope	Security
Cooperation	Humility	Simplicity
Courage	Humour	Success
Creativity	Inclusivity	Time
Curiosity	Independence	Tradition
Dignity	Initiative	Trust
Diversity	Integrity	Truth
Empowerment	Intuition	Wealth
Environment	Joy	Wellbeing
Efficiency	Justice	Wholeheartedness
Equality	Kindness	

And now, contemplate the following:

- Are you living to your values?

- What relationships do you want to nurture based on your values?

- What do you want your life to be about?

- What is your Vision and how will your values support you achieving this?

- What would you like your legacy to be?

- Where are you not living to your values?

- Think of a time when you were struggling. What values were you struggling to express in these moments?

- Who are you in your life?

- Who do you want to be?

The magical realisation I'd love you to get here is that to live in integrity and *to live in alignment with our core values is to live a life of Meaning and Purpose* that will fuel our Abundance is all areas of our lives. For the richness we feel when we are in alignment with our Values nourishes and enriches our lives, our relationships, our communities, our sense of belonging, our sense of self-worth, and our value in our world. Moreover, it allows us to be part of something bigger than ourselves. This is wealth *from the inside* out and the extra-beautiful thing about it is that it creates a ripple effect, radiating outwards with each action we take and each connection we make. Like a pebble dropped in a pond our influence expands, creating a series of outward increasing circles of inspiration and impact. This is a very real, and oh-so priceless, side effect of living in alignment with our core values.

Living from and with our values allows us to thrive, and if adversity comes knocking, we have the resilience and gumption to get through it and to flourish. This thriving through adversity is known as post traumatic growth in positive psychology, meaning we learn in spite of adversity *and* because of it.

RECOGNISING STRENGTH IN ADVERSITY

I'd like you to reflect back on a difficult or challenging time in your past. Choose a time or situation which you can now see in hindsight had a silver lining, and where your life actually changed for the better because of it. When situations, people or events are hard to bear, it's not always clear at the time how it can be strengthening us, but there are always lessons and insights to find.

I've worked with clients who have used this reflective exercise to see where a relationship, whether personal or business, fell apart, and often they observe that the 'bad thing' that happened was actually the best thing for them, because they went on to meet their Soul mate or to create a more spiritually-aligned business, making more of a difference in the world than they would have if the previous venture had succeeded.

Sometimes these changes in direction are more like a nudge from the Universe to adjust our sails and set off to new horizons.

Take a moment to journal on these above-mentioned questions or go into contemplation if you prefer.

YOUR MANIFESTO

Now let's create your personal or professional living manifesto based on your values. You can get as creative as you like and have fun with this too.

1. What are your core values and how will you ensure you living by them? What does this look like for you? For example, one of

my core values is honesty and for me I ensure this shows up in how I communicate both personally and professionally. I will only accept people into my space who also share this value. I will only work and collaborate with people who choose honesty over manipulation and BS. You can make this about life or work.

2. What are you committed to?

3. What is the essence to how you live and show up that is woven through everything you do?

4. What are the variations on the ways your values can show up for you? Freedom is important to me and this can show up in my love of travel. I love to travel for adventure, new experiences and new connections, and I integrate this value into my professional life by running retreats in places like Italy, Hawaii and Scotland. On these retreats, everything we do has a light-hearted fun element to it, even when we go deep into the inner work. We don't need to weigh ourselves down, or our clients, as we navigate stormy waters. That's another way I live my value of freedom.

Variations: Ways this can show up for me

You can go a step further with creating your manifesto like I did here with this creation made in Canva. I added travel, Spiritual, out of the box thinking, and adapted honesty to be 'real talk no BS'. This was inspired by working with Shari Teigman who has coined the phrase 'Woo & Do' (so cool right), and Marianne Cantwell. I share this Canva template below in our community circle for this book at www.ionarussell.com/elemental-circle. Come and join us here.

CHAPTER 15

Reflections & Suggestions: Know Thyself

1. Implementing more Joy into your life using your own Joy Jigsaw will boost your well-being and raise your own vibration. You can further boost your vibes by adding in small pockets of positivity into your day. Think of three areas that you need to raise the vibe and come up with some creative ways to lift the mood. You might choose when you wake up, or when you're on the way to work, or before bed, and add juicy ginger shots of positivity. Brainstorm some creative ideas. For example, if you don't like the journey to work you could create an epic playlist and listen to it on your commute.

2. Professor Barbara Fredrickson's studies on love and a variety of other positive emotions like Joy, inspiration, and gratitude are covered in her book *Positivity*, printed by One World Publications. If you'd like to dive into some more reading, she has a lot of great books and articles out there.

3. I've mentioned *The Art of Contemplation: Gentle path to wholeness and prosperity* by Richard Rudd a few times, and I recommend you check it out. It's printed by Gene Key publishing. I have been lucky enough to interview Richard on my radio show *WTF Conscious Collective*, Season 1 episode 4, which you can find on my website under 'Radio Shows and Podcasts', aka my speakers' corner.

4. Richard Knight, my friend, and co-facilitator of exclusive live events and retreats, is the 'Mozart of modern tarot', teaching his own unique methods in his own masterclass. If you would like to learn more about training with Richard Knight for your

Tarot and Psychic Development check out his website www. richard-knight.co.uk

5. You can find out more about mine and Richard's joint events and retreats, where we guide and amplify your intuition, your spiritual gifts and activate your real magic, by checking out our websites for upcoming dates. At the time of writing, we have retreats running in Europe, starting with Florence, Paris and London in 2023.

6. Breathwork: I love and have trained in the Pranayama Breathing also known as connected breathing with Jesse Gross at www.breathworkhealings.com Now, he's a very cool, unique, and inspired Heart-centred adventurer, coach, and author, who goes where the wild things are! Do check him out, he's based in LA and facilitates many adventures to places far and wide, including Nepal, and Peru, and he also runs retreats in the USA in the deserts and under wise old trees. www.JesseGros.com

7. However you choose to tune into your intuition, I invite you to keep notes on your phone or in a journal. You will start to see patterns and gain insight into what works best for you. I still find old journals and I am often amazed that what I wrote has come to be a few years later.

8. I've worked with Shari Teigman and Marrianne Cantwell, both of whom who I mentioned in the previous chapter, in a program called Rise in 2020. Shari is a creative strategist and performance maverick mentor who works with non-average Joes and Janes to unleash their inner Maverick and to remove the bottlenecks that keep them stuck and small to catapult them into the next level of fulfilment and success in all areas of life and business. Her website is shariteigman.com. Marianne has a book called *Be A Free Range Human: Escape the 9-5, Create a Life You Love and Still Pay the Bills*, published by Kogan Page. You can find out more about her at free-range-humans.com

9. Canva Template for your manifesto is available in our community circle at www.ionarussell.com/elemental-circle

10. Here are some assessments that I love and really help you to know what drives you, what you value and how you express love. They all offer free tests. Use your search engine to find Value in Action survey (VIA), the Gallop Strength assessment, and Love Language Quiz. Explore these and celebrate your strengths rather than trying to work harder on what isn't in your zone of genius. I hope you, like my clients, find these eye-opening and that they empower you to uncover your secret sauce. Sometimes the things you have been told are 'too much' about you or told to hide away are exactly what you need to bring out into the light. Let's get our freak on and celebrate.

PART 3: WATER

Reflection

CHAPTER 16

The Water Principle

WATER *represents Emotional Release, Intuition, and Inner Reflection. The Energy of Healing Your Heart.*

Next, you'll break down the barriers and uncover and clear what truly limits you. This process of uncovering, releasing, and deep clearing will allow you to grow and move forward with your own Inner Wealth of Knowledge — and then create from that unique space.

> *"Water is the mirror that has the ability to show us what we cannot see. It is the blueprint for our reality, which can change with a single, positive thought. All it takes is faith if you're open to it."*
>
> — *Masaru Emoto*

To begin, consider what inspires you, and steers you forward. Likewise, what distracts or hinders you? At a basic level, these are your motivations and your limitations. We're going to explore in depth where these come from, and how we can clear and let go of what we no longer need to carry.

The truth is, you are the sum part of all those that came before you – and you are also your own unique Cosmic blueprint. I really don't want you to lose sight of the second half of that sentence as we make our way through these coming chapters, which are geared towards developing our awareness of why we are the way we are, and why we think the way we think.

We all harbour conscious and unconscious patterns and behaviours which determine how we navigate life. We pick these patterns up from our family environment, as well as the culture and society we live in. Interestingly, we can take on these ways of BEing without even knowing or wanting to do so. Our parents learned from their parents and culture, and their parents learned from their parents and culture... and so it goes back to the beginning of time.

What patterns and beliefs are you repeating? Whose are they, if not yours? As well as your immediate family and those who raised you, is it possible your beliefs are rooted in ancestors who lived hundreds of years ago? And could they also be the echo of a past life?

It is time to wash away all that has held you back until this moment, and become aware of your own strength and your own real magic.

MOON MANIFESTATIONS

Before we dive deeper, I'd be remiss not to discuss the moon as we step into the element of WATER.

Within WATER is all of life. Your magnificent human body is made up of 60% water, about 70% of the Earth's surface is covered by water, and the moon certainly plays a dance with the ever-changing tides.

The moon is considered to influence our mental and emotional healing, possessing feminine qualities like forgiveness, acceptance, surrender, and calmness when in balance. Understanding the moon and its phases is a wonderful way to tap into and work with intention, manifestation, releasing/letting go, inner work, and personal growth.

Have you noticed any differences in your levels of vitality or your mood at different points of the lunar cycle? Perhaps you've sensed how the energy feels fresh and new with a new moon? And what about the high chaotic energy of a full moon?

A friend of mine worked in emergency services for years and she often shared how on the full moon they tended to be a lot busier, calls were a lot more 'out there', and human behaviours were a little crazier than normal.

I found while working in the service industries (bars and restaurants) that a Saturday full moon was the most intense to work, with drunken antics often amplified and some people acting a little irrational. Hello to any werewolves in the house!

We can tap into this powerful moon and WATER energy and flow with it, forgiving, washing away, and releasing that which no longer serves us. We can tap into our deeper knowing to call in that which will lift us up, letting go of any beliefs that aren't actually ours, and make manifest what we are here to create from our own Cosmic blueprint.

Check out where the moon is in her cycle and grab your journal tonight. The moon is a wonderful collaborator for intention setting. Here are some guidelines on what to channel and journal.

Full Moons are considered the most powerful because the moon is at her fullest and has reached completion. It is the most natural time to take stock of what no longer serves you and how you can create space for something better to come in. It is a wonderful time to release stagnant or negative energy. In releasing you make space for new to come in.

Write your intentions for:

- Clearing out energy

- Releasing outdated beliefs

- Letting go of old baggage

This is also a great time to cleanse your house. Clear out clutter to make room for the new energies to come in.

New Moons are considered the best time to go inwards and look to start anew with a clean slate.

Write your intentions for:

- Starting a new chapter

- Beginning new ventures or projects

- Supporting your inner work and shadow work

- Personal growth

- Personal development

Other moon phases

- **Waxing moon**: best for creative work, inspiration, and intention-setting

- **Waning moon**: best for forgiveness, letting go, giving thanks, releasing, and grounding

- **Blue moon**: best for goals, ambitions, aspirations, and celebrations

As I've mentioned, journaling is a powerful positive psychological tool to support your overall wellbeing. You can choose to work with the moon by writing your intentions in a notebook, or on a piece of paper to burn when you've finished. If you choose to burn and release your intentions to the moon energies, please do so safely and have WATER to hand to pour over the ashes. BE safe!

When journaling, honour your own intuitive insights and let yourself free flow without concern for grammar or spelling. Allow the thoughts, feelings, and emotions of your true desires to show up. Give gratitude to yourself for giving yourself this gift.

CHAPTER 17

Thoughts and Beliefs

"Water is the softest thing, yet it can penetrate mountains and earth. This shows clearly the principle of softness overcoming hardness."

— *Lao Zi*

As we discovered in Chapter 12, we have 80,000 thoughts a day. Of those, 80% are negative and 95% are exactly the same repetitive thoughts as the day before.

This blows my mind.

Take a second to consider what thoughts have dominated your thinking time so far today. What concerns, plans, presumptions, apprehensions, expectations, hopes, or judgements have been present in your mind?

Thoughts become things. And so it's vitally important that we become aware of where we're placing our attention. Everything begins with a thought, and our thoughts influence the words we speak and the actions we take — which, of course, is what creates our life experiences and the reality we are living in.

Our attitudes to our circumstances reflect our perceptions. As the great late Wayne Dyer said, "Change the way you look at things, and the things you look at change". I had this pinned up on the wall behind my computer when I was navigating life after the divorce. It became a beautiful reminder that I could choose how to look at things, think about things, and respond to things.

Our thoughts are like a garden, what we water flourishes, and what we ignore withers.

So what are you paying attention to with your thoughts?

"What the thinker thinks, the prover proves," as noted by the author Robert Anton Wilson in his book *Prometheus Rising*. In other words, your mind just wants to prove whatever you have chosen to think or believe about reality, to keep you safe in what is familiar to you. This is the magic of your beautiful mind. Which totally has your back, but doesn't always like to break through the comfort zone barrier or let go of the limiting beliefs that are on repeat in your mind like a broken record player.

A really simple way to play with this concept is to take a walk and set the intention at the start that you will see or experience beautiful things on your walk. Really expect, believe, and assume you will see beautiful things. You'll find yourself paying more attention to what's around you, and noticing things you wouldn't if you were in a different mindset. You might see something not traditionally perceived as 'beautiful', like a slug or snail, but you'll appreciate or even marvel at its slow, sleek movements, or the intricate patterns on its shell.

This one small example demonstrates both Wayne Dyer's and Robert Anton's words:

What the thinker thinks, the prover proves.

Change the way you look at things and the things you look at change.

I find this both revelatory and empowering, and I hope you do too.

And yet, just being told to 'think differently' isn't always enough. It's not always quite that simple. Awareness is key.

One thought *does* have the power to change everything – but your mind wants to protect you. To keep you safe in the cave, safe from what's unknown and lurking around the corner. In other words, to keep you safe from what the mind perceives as danger.

Acknowledging this, and the fact that we all have a lot of programming running on automatic pilot is essential as we begin to unpick, release and let go of the thoughts that don't serve us.

WHO'S RUNNING THE SHOW?

The automatic programming running in the background of your unconscious accounts for about 90% of your thinking and is the foundation for many of your behaviours, habits, and beliefs, as well as your sense of identity and your self-worth.

Your conscious awareness is only responsible for about 10% of your thoughts, and it's those thoughts that are more logical and calculated. It's where we plan out our strategies in life, and our goals, make our linear plans, and take aligned measurable action.

The unconscious is the stuff hidden below the surface. This is also where our intuition and emotions hang out. In essence, the unconscious houses the aspects of us that are running the show.

Such as our:

- Individual paradigms

- Habits

- Cultural beliefs

- Basic identity

- Basic beliefs

- Specific beliefs

- Fears of failure

- Fears of success

- Sense of self-worth

- Assumptions

- Projections

- Need for belonging

- Loyalty to parents/family

Are you curious about what — or who — is governing these programs? Is it time to dive a little deeper, and from there claim your sovereignty?

YOU ARE WHO YOUR GRANDMOTHERS PRAYED FOR: YOU ARE HERE

We've looked at how our thoughts and beliefs influence and impact our reality, now I'd like you to consider:

Are your thoughts and beliefs really 'your' thoughts and beliefs?

What ancestral memories might you be carrying, in your physical DNA and in your memories?

And what about our Soul energetic memories, generated from our past lives? There's more coming up on that subject in Chapter 18.

Let's start by considering the physical DNA that makes you up. The genetic stuff. As I'm sure you've gathered by now, I love a bit of number crunching so brace yourselves!

Most of us are aware of how our parents' attitudes and perceptions influenced us. Even if we choose not to share those attitudes and perceptions, they still had a huge impact on us. But we have to go back further than one generation. As I noted several pages ago, your parents had parents who had parents who had parents... and each of these relationships has had an effect on you, and made you who you are this very minute.

Let's go back 400 years and take a look at your family tree. Taking average numbers, ages, and lifespans, 400 years equates to twelve generations, and twelve generations equate to:

- 4094 people

- 127 romantic encounters to make you

- 254 parent-child relationships

- 252 in-law relationships

That's a lot of people, connections, and relationships. But what were those relationships like? Kind and loving, angry and contentious, generous and giving or miserly and jealous?

Now you're beginning to see why it's relevant to consider our physical, ancestral roots: because we are the daughters and sons of those that came before us.

It makes you wonder, whose beliefs are you living by?

What are your thoughts on money and wealth? What about entrepreneurial ventures vs working 9-5? What do you think and believe about family, success, happiness, joy?

And are these your beliefs, or those of your great-great-great-great grandmother Mabel?

What lessons and behaviours are in your family line, passed down from generation to generation? What challenges did your grandparents face that manifest in how you relate to obstacles now? How much unconditional love did they experience that is felt in your Heart? How much sadness, neglect or destitution did they endure that you feel in your bones? Did they find happiness or sadness as their default setting? Did they prosper easily or work their fingers to the bone?

The beautiful thing is you can look to your family and observe the lessons, patterns, and behaviours that are your family traits, your unconscious programming ... *and choose to let them go.*

I have so many stories I could share about clients who have uncovered and let go of limiting beliefs inherited from their families, from a woman who held deep shame for how her father treated their servants in Africa – and went on to accept and no longer hide from her wealth; to another who let go of trauma at the hands of those in authority — and went on to find self-worth, self-Love and spiritual confidence; to many others who realised they needed to acknowledge a lack of Love in their pasts before learning to Love themselves — and are now in loving relationships.

Personally, I grew up witnessing my father fail at entrepreneurial ventures and lose everything, and be incredibly tight fisted with money. He was a very demanding father who did the best he could with what he knew. My mother, on the other hand, showered us with unconditional Love, was incredibly generous and ran a flourishing café in Canada. I have invested a lot of time to working through my conflicting issues and noticing whose behaviours I have exhibited at times, letting go of those behaviours and patterns that no longer serve me. And this is just my parents. My Grandparents on both sides were so different again.

As you can see this is a multi-layered process, but with awareness comes growth and healing.

In a few pages time, we're going to explore Inner child work. You'll find it isn't always about uncovering a deep thread or pattern of behaviour, sometimes it's about recognising an incidental incident, often something seemingly small. Here's a couple of examples from my own experience, which I'm sharing here as they also point to how the limiting beliefs we have as adults can grow from the smallest of seeds planted in our younger years.

As a child, I remember singing at the top of my lungs with carefree abandon – until my friend innocently laughed at me. From that moment on I told myself I couldn't sing and that if I did, I'd be laughed at. Now, I'm not gonna say I now sing like a songbird, but I'm telling you this little anecdote to show how that one comment made me decide I'd never sing in public again. I'm glad to say I was able to uncover that and let it go. I'm not Beyoncé, but I sing from my Heart as if I was. I even joined a choir briefly for people who technically thought they couldn't sing. We were rather good, and what we lacked in skill we made up for in enthusiasm.

I also started down the path of an eating disorder based on an innocent comment by another friend who said she'd rather be fat and happy like me, than thin and miserable. I had never thought about my weight until that point. I was thirteen. There were obviously other issues at play, but that is the moment that I remember first viewing myself as fat. In fact, I was beautiful and I weighed less than I do now.

In short, I've witnessed so many light-bulb moments, as well as unfolding deep realisations, when clients have taken the step to explore where their limiting beliefs have come from. If you're interested in exploring this, please keep reading for more on how to tap into your awareness in this area.

FINDING YOUR TRUTH

What's coming up for you as you're reading this chapter? Take time out to journal or contemplate the questions I've posed so far. There's no rush, this is all a practice in Self-awareness and as I've said before there is no right way or wrong way to do this. Are you becoming aware of certain patterns of behaviour you may have picked up from how you were raised, or from your longer family line? Can you sense any limiting beliefs you might have inherited?

Write a list of any beliefs, awarenesses or insights that are popping up for you.

Feel into remembering where you heard these beliefs, these stories that you've taken in. And remember there's a link between our thoughts and what we see and experience in the world. Often, we are all just making stories up to fit into our perception of the world.

What if those stories are not yours, and not real or true for you?

And now, in contrast to the list of inherited limiting beliefs you've just created, consider the what about the list of beliefs below; read through these statements and notice how you feel.

- Life is magical

- Synchronicities happen for me all the time

- Everyone can be successful

- People are inherently good and want the best for each other

- Life is beautiful, abundant, and filled with Meaning and Purpose

- Everyone is a blessing

- There is a Higher Power that Loves and supports my growth

- There is a Source of Eternal Love

- We are all connected as One and I am never alone

- My Dreams will come True

- All I need to do is take aligned inspired action from my Heart and Life will unfold in Magical ways

As you read those statements, did you feel good, or doubtful? Excited, or daunted? Can those beliefs, which are not limiting, but expansive and full of possibility, be True for you?

This exercise isn't about accepting that these statements are accurate just because I say they are. This isn't about you bypassing what you naturally feel to be true or untrue.

This is about letting go of any narratives you're carrying of what 'they' — whoever 'they' are for you — said you should be, or how you should show up, or what is important, or what your worth is in the world.

It's about finding where you are – beyond your inherited beliefs. I always ask my clients to consider if their thoughts are empowering or disempowering and to look at them without judgment. Starting to notice the patterns in this is a beautiful first step.

Start uncovering your Truth, then we get to work from right where you are. This is where the Inner work begins.

HEALING THE INNER CHILD

You are in the midst of one of the most healing and restorative voyages a human being can choose to embark upon. The return to your path (or Inner Wellspring of self worth, prosperity and inner knowledge) is forming before you, with each new step you take. You have examined and reflected on how you grew up within your family and your culture, and that brings us beautifully to the child that you were when you began to observe, learn, and conform to the world around you.

There is so much magic and potential power in inner child work. It gives us a deeper understanding of our beliefs about ourselves, our place in the world around us, who we are and our Authentic Heart's Life Path. By resolving, listening, and healing our inner child we can let go of the past and the limits it may have placed on our own Inner Power.

There are many protocols served by many healers and therapists who work with inner child healing. One size does not fit all and your experiences have made you who you are; every method utilised in healing must be tailored to mend the wounds from your own personal journey.

Know this: you were born magnificent and magical, believing and trusting that the world is a good place.

Your inner child's belief systems were formed from birth up to between the ages of seven to twelve and then accepted into your unconscious as facts based on your experiences, both positive and negative, of how you see yourself in the world. This is not to say that all our beliefs are written by age seven or so; we continue to grow and evolve as we age, picking up information as we go. Our minds are neuroplastic, pliable, and malleable, not fixed and hardwired. As I've said, change your thoughts, change your life.

I'm frequently asked why childhood emotional repression can manifest itself in adulthood, often as anxiety, depression, or anger management issues. One of the analogies I use to explain this conflict is to imagine a splinter in the bottom of your foot. Initially, ignoring the discomfort of the splinter may be less painful than removing it. However, the longer the splinter is left in the skin, the more painful removal may become. Childhood emotional repression causes psychological wounds that inner child work helps to uncover, identify, and treat.

Inner child work does not have to be scary or painful to be effective; it can be safe, supportive, and empowering.

The key to unlocking healing is working with your unconscious programming to relieve learned behaviours and coping mechanisms, using techniques that are restorative and releasing, returning you to the elevation of joy and gratitude in your daily life. Think of this just like the factory reset function on your mobile phone.

Try this: Mindful meditation, both passive and active, can be used to help retrieve memories that have been buried deep in the subconscious due to pain and hurt. The writing of letters to your childhood self aids in the recalling of feelings of innocence, excitement, and joy that were present before any trauma occurred.

To begin either method (meditation or letter writing), when you have dropped into your Heart space and quietened your mind, you can ask questions to your inner child such as:

- How do you feel?

- How can I support you?

- What do you need from me?

Be patient with yourself and the aspect of yourself that is your inner child. You are creating a safe space for yourself to be heard, and if this part of you hasn't felt safe for a long while it might take a little time for your inner child to feel supported.

Internalising positive words of affirmation and kindness can be used during inner child healing work as a comfort from Elder-Self to the young Self. These phrases are usually simple, but powerful, and can include: *I see you, I hear you, and I Love you*.

The key here is in acknowledging your inner child, and those aspects or parts of you that maybe didn't feel heard, validated, worthy, secure or safe in the past, and listen to what that part of you needs. I refer to 'parts' not to disassociate these aspects, but more so that we can see we are human and whole, made of many complex pieces. One client, when she caught herself getting frustrated or angered, would just drop into her Heart with the 4 Elemental Heart Method and ask, "What am I needing in this moment?" and wait for the insight. For her, it was to feel heard, and she would listen to herself and acknowledge that this is what she needed. This applied in her personal and professional interactions.

Now it may not always be practical to pause like this in a meeting or heated discussion, but there is always time for a breath. And if you are regularly doing the Elemental Heart Activation you can more easily drop in with one conscious breath, and collect your thoughts. A pause is magical. Think of this as practical magic.

Many of the CEOs running big companies are still making snap decisions from their wounded child. Imagine this: a three year old who is resentful for not being heard in their family is making huge financial business decisions, or navigating their relationships with their staff from that wounded space.

The beautiful truth is: we all get to heal.

And imagine what the world would be like if we did. If we all knew how to make decisions from our Heart-centred adult self with Grace, Joy, and Compassion and coming from a place of self Love, self Belief and self Worth. Now that is a world I want to be part of. How about you?

You might want to return to the Joy Jigsaw process we covered in Chapter 11 and get creative with the things that bring your inner child joy. Painting, singing, playing, being silly — whatever it is. Give yourself permission to have fun with this part of you and bring innocent joy to your life today.

A little side note is that I appreciate that not all childhoods were safe and joyful, if this is you then I invite you to find the parts, no matter how small, that might have been lighter, and plant these like seeds. Seek support and allow yourself to rise up and grow/flourish.

WHAT'S THE STORY?

Next, I'd like you to take a deep dive into your recent family history, the stuff you can remember and are aware of. This is definitely an exercise you want to do with your journal by your side; it can be really revelatory.

Take some time to consider what was modelled around you. In particular, what did you see and hear about these topics:

- *Relationships and family*

- *Health and the body*

- *Money and finances*

- *Success and work*

Common relationship stories many kids pick up from adults might go along the lines of: *Everyone cheats, all marriages end in divorce, men are terrible, women are terrible, relationships steal your freedom...* and so on.

Health, in particular the body, is another area rife with judgments and limiting beliefs. You might have heard messages like: *If you're not thin you're lazy and greedy, it's shameful to show your body, being overweight is unattractive, men must be tall and muscly...*

Money is a huge subject for pretty much everyone, whether you had heaps of it or not. Think back and consider what you heard about money in your home, from peers, or on TV.

Take a look and see if you recognise any of the very common money mindsets, or limiting beliefs, listed below. I call them 'limiting beliefs' because they limit our perception and box us into a 'fixed' constricted mindset, rather than an expansive 'anything is possible' Abundant mindset. Here they are:

- *Money doesn't grow on trees*

- *Rich people are mean*

- *The likes of us can't do that*

- *Money is the root of all evil*

- *I'm unlucky with money*

- *There is never enough*

Something else to consider is: what does success look like to you and how was it modelled in your family? Some common stories around success are:

- *You have to work your fingers to the bone*

- *You have to work hard to succeed*

- *No one in our family is ever successful*

- *If you don't go to university, you won't succeed*

- *You'll never make money being creative*

- *Being entrepreneurial is a fool's game and too risky*

Are any of those familiar to you? Maybe in your family, the focus was on being an entrepreneur, working in corporate, or being self-employed. Or perhaps it was about how you can't be successful as an artist, musician, writer, or something else creative.

Are you starting to recognise how many stories we were subjected to when we were growing up, stories we have then taken on as our own?

These beliefs and ways of thinking can feel rooted and fixed, like they're facts or just the way it is for 'the likes of us'. However, let's flip this and consider that as we know our minds can grow, evolve, and change — then we can choose to adopt the perspective of a growth mindset.

In positive psychology, there's an emphasis on moving from a fixed mindset to a growth mindset.

Someone with a fixed mindset sees things as rigid and written in stone, and often views life as fatalistic, believing they have no control over outcomes.

A person with a growth mindset is open to the journey of possibility, change, and giving things a go. Those with a growth mindset bounce back from setbacks and feel in charge of their own lives.

Would you like to explore this further?

This intervention is inspired by the mindset work of Carol Dweck, along with Mel Deague's take on this in PPCA.

1. Journal on a negative experience, perception, or thought you have had around one of these areas:

   - Relationships

   - Health and the body

   - Money or finances

   - Success or work

2. Think about how the experience, your perception, and thoughts have played out in your life. Let's call this the story you have been living by.

3. What belief have you created about yourself based on this story?

4. Where did you first hear this story or belief? For example, if you're focusing on how you perceive money, what is your first memory of money, how was it expressed (spoken or implied), and by whom?

5. Have these stories or beliefs prevented you from doing something you really wanted to do? How and in what way?

6. How could your life be different if you let go of this story or belief?

7. What has this story enabled you to do, or how has it hindered you?

8. What have you learned from recognising this story and how can you use this experience to grow?

9. Now looking at the above story as the 'old story', how can you reframe and create a new story that will support your growth?

10. What are the aligned action steps you are going to take to reframe this belief?

11. Who would you be without the old belief, aka who will you BE with the new story?

12. What would you do differently with the new belief?

13. How will your life be different?

14. Who else's life will be different? How does this make you feel?

Side Note: If you find yourself judging the old story, I invite you to look at the feelings that accompany this judgment and come up with a less negative and more objective description of the experience in step 1, and then work through it from this less negative perspective.

Bonus note: Before we move on, I just want to quickly touch on something that ties in with the subject of the stories that we live by or tell ourselves. There's a term I want to share with you: the act of 'catastrophising'. Essentially this is when we think the worst of any situation. A quick example would be the way how many of us feel when someone hasn't responded to a text message we've sent, or when a social media post hasn't got the likes or comments that we want. In both of these examples, we're looking outside of ourselves for validation — and when we don't get that validation, we think of worst-case scenarios, such as *No one appreciates me*, or *I'm so unpopular*. When we do this, we give value to external unknown and made-up stories — and this only breeds anxiety.

Please be aware of the stories you are telling yourself. It is up to you to tell the stories that empower and free you.

As I shared earlier: our thoughts are like a garden, what we WATER flourishes, what we ignore withers. We might think the grass is greener on the other side of the fence; it isn't. It's greener where you WATER it.

What are you choosing to WATER in the garden of your Mind, Heart, and Soul?

CHAPTER 18

Messages from the Past

"We're all ghosts. We all carry, inside us, people who came before us."

— Liam Callanan, The Cloud Atlas

The EARTH and all her elements remember all that came before and all that will come after, for there is no time, no past, no future, it's all now in the present. The memories all rest within her and within us; we are connected to all life patterns both remembered and forgotten. We can access what has passed and gain the insight of what might be. By tuning in we can connect with our ancestors on all timelines.

To embrace the possibility of accessing all timelines, we must let go of linear thinking about what time is and allow the possibility that all time is happening now, in a spiral or a vortex, and that there is no separation between past, present, and future — there is only now.

If this is getting a bit out there for you, let's consider our dream state which has no linear time about it. We can be running around with mythical creatures, travelling in a time machine, and having dinner with Cleopatra. So if you can dispel disbelief and follow along here, trusting anything that comes through as true for you, then you might have some unexpected fun. I've witnessed some extraordinary journeys with my clients using these processes, and the magic is real. You never know where the golden nuggets are hidden.

OUR ANCESTRAL MEMORIES,
ON ALL TIMELINES

*"Without birth and death, and without the perpetual
transmutation of all the forms of life, the world would be
static, rhythm-less, undancing, mummified."*

— Allan Watts

What ancestral memories do we carry in our Soul's energetic memories?

Have you ever wondered if you've been here before?

Have you ever experienced flashbacks of memories that you do not recognise as your own?

Or do you have an unexplained fascination with another culture, a different time, or a unique interest that's out of sync with your birth family's norm?

The concept of reincarnation and past lives has been observed, both verbally and in written form, dating back as far as the history of man. Reincarnation is the rebirth of energy that occurs after a Soul has transitioned in death, manifesting itself in a new life. These lives are often not connected in any way and are not bound by physical characteristics such as race, age, gender, or location.

You might have the sense that there are skills or abilities you could uncover from a previous life to help you live your life now, or perhaps there are experiences from past incarnations showing up as residual energy that you'd like to clear and let go of.

Or you might just have a flicker of curiosity right now, and be interested in exploring the possibility of reincarnation with an open mind.

And, here's the really paradigm-shifting part: you might not have lived those lives yet. This is what I mean when I say we can access all timelines, and everything is happening now, in this rich and expansive moment.

Before I go on, I'd like you to know that if you do choose to explore the possibility of past or future lives, you can decide to look at what you discover as truth, or you can perceive what you learn as a metaphor for the answers that you seek. Your perception of this is 100% your own.

This is your journey, your dance, you are the conductor of your orchestra, and you get to choose the symphony that resonates with your Heart. I simply suggest you go for the rhythms that inspire you to higher vibrations of opportunity and anything that connects you to a deep feeling of fullness and abundance.

REGRESSION: THE KEY TO UNLOCKING OUR PAST OR FUTURE LIVES

The journey to discovering our Life or Soul Purpose is often filled with uncertainty and doubt, and regression therapy can provide clarity and guidance for those who are on a path towards discovering their ultimate Purpose and the Legacy we are here to birth. I'd like to share my experience as a past life regression therapist with you here, and give you a sense of what exploring our past lives can bring to the magnificent unfolding of your current one.

"Until you make the unconscious conscious, it will direct your life and you will call it fate."

— Carl Jung

The process of regression is one synonymous with deep relaxation. The total release of physical and mental tension is encouraged, removing the barriers to repressed thoughts and memories. From a state of tranquillity, you are guided through a series of questions aimed at revealing any other lives you have lived or will live. Contrary to popular belief, regression clients do not lose consciousness during their sessions. They maintain full control of their senses and have the freedom to end the session at any point.

Similar to the inner child work mentioned in the previous chapter, regression requires us to be mindfully open to the process of releasing energy and allowing our awareness to wander. It is important to begin a session with an understanding of the questions you would like answered and a strong, clear intention.

A relaxing, safe, and transformational calm space is created, and from this meditative space, you can access felt Soul memories, the revelation of a calling, or a liberation from negative thoughts. This type of process can be beneficial even for those who do not believe in past lives. Regressions often lead to life lessons through subconscious metaphors and parallels that can be applied to present situations.

I've guided many clients through this process and am so often amazed at its transformative power. Those with unexplainable anxiety and phobias have realised there's a connection between how they feel now and the events they experienced in other lives. Some have felt the meditative process of regression as a deep healing journey, often uncovering a metaphorical story. One such client saw herself galloping on a horse across a misty beach wearing an early 19th-century corset, her petticoats billowing behind her as she fled from a male figure who she felt was suppressing her expression. As we dived into her experience she was overcome with emotion and felt it was a sign to break free from her current career choice and live a more fulfilling life setting down the bondage of a patriarchal system (the corset). She reinvented herself and her career providing inspirational mindset workshops at the corporate level rather than conforming as an employee within her previous role.

These methods of exploration do not need to be a traumatising or stressful to be effective. Each life discovered can contain both joyful and painful experiences; the power of the process comes as we learn how those experiences affect the beliefs and behaviours of our current journey. The visualisations and emotions that are experienced in the theatre of the mind are manifestations stemming from our own subconscious.

Whether or not you believe in the concept of reincarnation and past or future lives, regression therapy is a useful tool for identifying the root of negative emotions. It is common for us to mentally bury trauma and grief rather than facing them directly and employing healthy coping mechanisms. The regression process often unveils these badly-concealed emotional wounds and provides the avenue through which this harmful energy can be released from the mind safely and without re-traumatisation.

Past life meditation is a full sensory experience; and you can commonly see, hear, feel, and smell the details of stories vividly as they unfold. Emotions such as grief, anger, joy, and love can often be felt so strongly that you feel you have been physically transplanted into the storyline of a past or future life. The exploration of negative life events may be necessary for certain types of breakthroughs, but this exploration is always done with the permission of the client and at a pace of their choosing. The goal is not to burden the client with the negative events of their other lives, but to allow them the safe navigation of these experiences for current life perspective.

I believe that past life processes and meditations are ideal for those who are questioning their life path and seeking clarity and direction, helping to uncover and to restore balance, focus, and enlightenment to your life.

It's your choice how you see this chapter. There is no right way or wrong way.

Is it a memory or is a metaphor for life?

Well, that's for you to decide. If you choose to explore regression therapy, find a skilled practitioner who you trust. If you're interested in trying a gentle but powerful process by yourself, I invite you to try this next exercise.

FREE WRITING
FOR INSIGHT AND REMEMBERING

We can tap into further insights by setting intentions for guidance and direction using this free-writing process. We set the intention to receive information on any gifts and positive attributes we have had that will empower us now for the greater good.

This is a very intimate meditation, and one that really works well as an audio. Grab a pen and paper and head to our free online community space to access a recording of me guiding you through this process at www.ionarussell.com/elemental-circle. You can read on for the instructions, but I do recommend you try the full sensory experience by listening to the audio.

For this practice, you're going to let the thoughts flow out of you without analysing them or correcting them. Forget grammar and spelling. Open up your intuitive flow through your Heart and unconscious pathways. Light incense or a candle if it is safe to do so. Sit in a comfortable position.

1. First, begin with the Heart Space Activation (Chapter 4). Feel your Heart as you continue.

2. Set your positive intention clearly for your meditation and be willing to intuitively tune into what you hear, sense, feel and sense for the rest of the meditation.

3. If you like you can play some drumming music or some deep theta rhythms.

4. Call in your guides, your healing, your support team, however this is for you. I will call them your guides for the rest of the exercise.

5. As you continue to breathe from your Heart, sense a white healing light radiating out from your Heart and enveloping you in Love and Light. Perhaps you see a colour, perhaps it is golden or white.

6. Sit here in this moment and be present to your intention for 10-20 minutes.

7. Imagine your guide walking with you at your side, towards a bridge. The bridge over the WATER of your unconscious awareness. Coming towards you is a messenger who represents your Higher Self, your Inner Knowing, your Higher Wisdom — and they have a message about your gifts, your positive attributes, that will help you in this lifetime. Be open to the gifts and insights with a Loving Heart and positive vibes.

8. Listen with all your senses. Allow this to be like a beautiful dream state.

9. When you are ready to come out of the meditation, bring your awareness back to the room and continue to focus on your Heart and breathe.

When you are ready open your eyes and start journaling. Remember not to be analytical or critical. Let the words flow. Perhaps you might describe images, draw shapes, squiggles, words, or sentences. Write from your beautiful Heart space in this relaxed moment.

See what insight you gain from the intention you set. You are intuitively tapping into your Inner Wisdom and intuition. You have everything you seek within you.

Tip: You can do a 'brain dump' before beginning this free-writing exercise if you feel your mind is buzzing. If you're wondering what the heck a brain dump is, then let me shine a light on the term. Perhaps your brain is restless, preoccupied, stressed, worried, locked in overthinking, or buzzing with ideas or to-do lists. When that's the case, I invite you to literally dump the contents of your brain out onto paper. Kind of like when you empty the recycle bin on your computer. If we don't empty the recycle bin, all the contents are still there taking up space on the hard drive. You are quite literally clearing the WATERS of your mind. Think of a beautiful clear ocean that you want to swim in, versus murky WATERS littered with clutter.

CHAPTER 19

Forgiveness

"If you don't make peace with your past, it will keep showing up in your present."

— *Wayne Dyer*

In my experience, all journeys of Self-discovery include healing, and from what I've learnt and witnessed, a huge part of the journey of Self-discovery happens when we forgive ourselves and others. And there's no better time to explore this than now because there's a good chance that the process of travelling through the element of WATER has brought things to the surface for you that you will need to let go of in order to move forward.

Harry Uhane Jim, the writer of *Wise Secrets of Aloha*, says you have two choices: "You can forgive now or forgive later."

If you're holding onto resentment, guilt, shame, anger, or sadness, you are holding onto fear and limiting your ability to create the life you want free from the ties that bind you to the past. Those dense feelings will cloud your own Inner Knowing and confuse your Inner Wisdom. It's all baggage, and baggage is heavy and will rob you of energy.

Lack of forgiveness is much like a roadblock on the path to Prosperity and Peace of mind and the life you want. It's the result of judging yourself or others. By holding onto the past, you hold onto fear which is a low vibrational energy. In Chapters 12, 15, and 26 we touched on the emotional vibration scale and fear is at the bottom part of this scale.

We all need a clear and clean space to listen to our intuition — which, as we discovered in EARTH Part 2, is our very own superpower. To do this, we must shift our attention, and forgive any transgressions of ourselves or others.

When you learn to let go of judgement, you can forgive and move forward, replacing the negativity with Love rather than fear. Only then can you let go of the victim mentality and be empowered with Love.

Now we are all human here (or so I presume), and I am not telling you to override and ignore your feelings. It is human to judge, but don't get angry at yourself for anything you discover here. Instead, choose to move forward with awareness.

Ask yourself, Am I living from a place of Love or Fear?

As we've explored, wherever we focus is where our energy is directed, and we'll attract more of the same. If we judge ourselves and others, we'll invite more situations into our life that will cause us to judge others or to be judged.

What do you want to attract into your life, more fear, or more Love? It's time to let fear go.

FORGIVENESS LETTER

The forgiveness letter is a proven positive psychological intervention which releases negative emotions and softens or eliminates distress caused by their psychological weight. Holding onto these feelings only hurts you, not the person you are feeling negative energy towards.

1. Think of someone that you feel resentment or other negative feelings towards (this can also be yourself) and write a forgiveness letter to them from your Heart Space. Avoid writing as a victim, which gives away your power.

2. Read through the letter, and notice if you are feeling forgiving or not. Why do you think this is?

3. You may choose to burn the letter and let it go with compassion. Remember to do this safely.

4. Afterwards, reflect on how it felt to write the letter and how it felt to burn it.

5. Ideally, you want to reach a place where you feel neutral about the person or incident. You are literally taking the energetic charge out of the situation.

You may notice ideas drop in throughout your day after you have done this, or any of the free-writing exercises in this book. So keep a pen and paper handy.

After this exercise, you might begin to feel a lightness as if you have lightened the weight you were carrying. As you let go and move on, you might feel more loving in general, like a warm fuzzy glow feeling in your Heart. Do you remember the scene in *How The Grinch Stole Christmas* by Dr. Seuss where the Grinch starts to have feelings? "The Grinch's small Heart grew three sizes that day". Allow feelings in and through. It's nourishing. We gotta feel it to heal it. (I used to read *The Grinch* to my son for so many nights that I know it off by Heart. I can't tell you the page this is from — I just know it by Heart!)

CHAPTER 20

Reflections & Suggestions: Water Element

1. If your interest has been sparked by the quote of Masaru Emoto, then you can find out more online, and my favourite book of his, *The Hidden Messages in Water*, is published by Atria Books.

2. To find out the upcoming moon phases search moongiant.com for a full lunar calendar.

3. When moon journaling, notice how you feel about working with the moon phrases. You might find that the releasing and burning of the intentions is more powerful than straight journaling. It's interesting to notice what we notice. There is a lot to be gained in reflection of what we feel aligned with – or not, as the case might be. Remember it's up to you what you choose to practise and adopt into your ongoing processes or rituals.

4. In Chapter 17 I shared some 'Ancestral Mathematics' from familytree.com. Take a look at https://www.familytree.com/blog/you-are-here-because-of-1024-ancestral-lines/ where you will see a fabulous graphic to demonstrate the incredible number of ancestral lines we all have.

5. Stephen Galloza noted in *Faith, Hope, & Psychology, The Miracle Zone*, that "80 % of Thoughts Are Negative...95 % are repetitive". Published March 2, 2012, he also stated that "In 2005, the National Science Foundation published an article regarding research about human thoughts per day. The average person has about 12,000 to 60,000 thoughts per day. Of those, 95% are exactly the same repetitive thoughts as the day before and

about 80% are negative."

https://faithhopeandpsychology.wordpress.com/2012/03/02/80-of-thoughts-are-negative-95-are-repetitive/

6. If you are drawn to the inner child work, I urge you to seek a professional that you resonate with. You must feel safe in their presence and trust them. There are many books written on this topic too. I use these processes within my 1-to-1 private work with clients which spans a number of months, or in a day-long immersive. If you'd like to find out about working with me please head to my website, ionarussell.com, and complete the contact form.

7. Carol Dweck is Professor of Psychology at Stanford University and is known for her work on mindset. She has a great many books you can jump into if you want to learn more about her work. I particularly like her book *Mindset - Changing The Way You Think to Fulfil Your Potential* published by Robinson.

8. Niyc Pidgeon, who wrote one of my forewords, is a Positive Psychologist, MSc, is Founder and Creator of The Positive Psychology Coach Academy Certification (PPCA). Mel Deague, Positive Psychologist, MSc, is the PPCA Curriculum Lead. You can find out more about getting certified as a Positive Psychology Coach at https://niyc-pidgeon.mykajabi.com/positive-psychology-coach-academy-1

9. More on catastrophising www.psychologytoday.com/gb/basics/catastrophizing

10. If you would like to explore past lives more there are some great books written by Dr. Brian Weiss. My favourite is *Many Lives, Many Masters* published by Simon and Schuster. Perhaps your curiosity has been sparked further, if so, you can look into some of the works of Michael Newton Ph.D. and Delores Cannon as a starting place.

11. Harry Uhane Jim is the author of the book *Wise Secrets of Aloha*.

PART 4: AIR

Intention, Direction & Flow

CHAPTER 21

The Air Principle

AIR represents intellect, intention, and connection to Universal Life Source. The Energy of what is yet to be seen with the human eye, it's an inner Higher Wisdom. It is in constant movement and is barely noticeable to the human eye except when it is fierce and powerful. It is also refreshing and cleansing... think of blowing the cobwebs away to make room for what we are calling in.

Our exploration of AIR allows you to activate and connect with your Powerful Vision, setting and tuning in to it as your own personal compass bearing. You will have a clear inspired path guided by The Energy of your Envisioned future to creating your Elementally Abundant life for the greater good of all. Now the Magic begins!

"Don't look for your dreams to come true: look to become true to your dreams."

— *Rev Michael Beckwith*

It is time to dance to the rhythms of your Soul's Purpose and uncover your own personal Vision. Just as the ancient Polynesian Wayfinders intuitively navigated across the seas reading the elements, you too can follow the course of your Heart and the stars on your horizon to discover what Authentic Happiness, Success, and Abundance means and looks like for you.

AIR is critical to life, and yet we can't see it. What we can see and feel are its effects: winds blow across our planet, the warm breeze comes in from the ocean, and cool gusts come down from the snow-covered caps. When a storm is brewing, there's a sudden and brutal squall. The tropical trade winds blow in from the north and drive ships forward across the oceans.

AIR is powerful. It moves us just as our thoughts and passions move us, calling us forward, drawing us towards the horizon of our Dreams.

How can we harness the element of AIR, to manifest the lives we Dream of?

Working with the AIR principle is about intellectually and emotionally stepping into and confidently embodying that which you are here to create. And while I'm not about to get all fluffy unicorns on you, I am asking you to trust that which you can't see. I am asking you to have Faith in yourself and the Magic of the Universe.

These chapters are a chance for you to get crystal clear on your Vision for you and your future so that you can follow that Vision and manifest it with intention and clarity.

When we create our life from clarity and ease, we open the AIR waves for opportunities to find us. Unexpected chances and spontaneously-aligned connections appear, as if by magic. This is where REAL MAGIC occurs.

For this, we need to be clear on what our Vision is. We need to be willing to know it and express it with an open Heart full of positive intention, gratitude, and in coherence with the greater good for all. The 'greater good for all' is key here: please never try to gain something at another's expense. If someone has what you desire, you can frame your Vision like this: "I'd like something like that, or greater than that which I know, and for the good of all."

Don't worry if you don't yet have a strong and specific sense of what your Vision is. That's why we're here, right now. In the next chapter, I have a powerful process to share with you called Your Vision Quest, and then I'll invite you to step into and embody that Vision with a practice known as Best Possible Self.

But perhaps you already know exactly what you want. You might even have a flicker of impatience because your Vision is clear and formed and you are raring to go. And while I love your enthusiasm, I also invite you to slow down and take the time to engage in the following exercises and activities. As you'll discover, it's not just about what we want to create — it's about understanding the level we're *living from* — and *therefore creating from*.

Perhaps you already have a deeply felt sense of your big Vision, and you are already living it. So I invite you to go deeper with it. There's always more growth and evolution in the up-levelling. None of us have arrived, and we are all on the journey. May we all lift the vibe of humanity together.

THE FOUR STAGES OF CONSCIOUS LIVING

Between you and your Vision are a thousand routes, some perilous, some smooth. Some have deviations, detours, and dangerous waters. Others are flowing, fluid, and fun! And faster, too. One of the ways we can hook up with that faster current is to consider our current level of consciousness because that's what will determine our route, and write our map.

There are different levels of consciousness available to us all, and this is something that's been explored by several new thought leaders. The context I particularly love is known as The Four Stages of Consciousness. The first time I came across this concept was through the works of Reverend Michael Bernard Beckwith, the founder of the nondenominational Ministry Agape in Los Angeles. He is a prolific writer, speaker, and spiritual thinker who's sat on Oprah's stage — which gives him a whole other level of credibility in our modern society.

Most people currently on the planet are in the first two stages of consciousness, but you might have experienced all four. It's useful to note that whatever stage we're in, we're not stuck there, and generally we flow between all four stages, as in a spiral.

Take a look at these descriptions and see which stage you think you are living your life in now. If you'd like to, consider how you can consciously make the changes to elevate to a higher level.

The four stages are:

1. TO **ME**. Victim consciousness: *Life is happening to me.*

   In this stage, there's a feeling of a lack of control and a belief that life is governed by external forces influencing your Joy, Happiness, Success and Prosperity. There's a lack of Purpose, and others are to blame for your circumstances.

   In this state your thinking might be:

   - I just can't get a break

   - Everyone else has an easier life

   - I am so unlucky nothing goes right for me

   You may also be in a stage of just needing to cope and survive, going through habitual motions, perhaps feeling that you're on a hamster wheel going nowhere.

   To move up from this stage you are invited to release blame, shame, and guilt and move into gratitude.

2. BY **ME**. Responsibility consciousness: *Life is happening by me.*

   Moving away from blame, you are now taking personal responsibility for your life. You are an achiever, you have a sense of empowerment and understand the principles of manifestation. You are in a state of creating life and are aware that you can choose how you react to outside forces. You are manifesting what you wish for and desire. Yippee! You know you can choose to create your life and your Purpose.

   There is a focus on personal ownership and personal growth and you might:

- Use your imagination and visualisation to create your reality

- Be striving to achieve

- Be working hard and sweating to make things happen

- Be determined and focused

- Be thinking, I did this, I created this, I made this happen...

- Be proactive, developing skills and strengthening your values

This stage is characterised by feeling like you are in control — but to keep evolving beyond here you need to be willing to surrender control. Control is an illusion anyway. Have you noticed the more you try to control something, the more stressed you can become? It's time to let go and surrender.

3. **THROUGH ME**. Surrender consciousness: *Life is happening through me.*

   Now you accept life happens through you, you are co-creating with The Universe, Source, Universal Consciousness — whatever your preferred term is for *Something greater than yourself*. There is a sense of flow and things happening easily. Many creatives, musicians, writers, and artists say their ideas just came to them as intuitive inspired insight. At this level you are:

- Heart-centred, with heightened intuition

- Focused on helping and supporting others

- Imaginative; creative ideas flow

- Open to receiving beyond your imagination

- No longer judging of others or the world

- More focused on Soul Goals and Life Purpose

To move beyond here is to let go of feeling separate from these higher forces and to feel connected to everything … to be as one with everything, and nothing.

4. AS **ME**. Oneness consciousness: *Life happens as me.*

    You feel that you are one with the Universe and you embody Truth. This is a Spiritual experience in pure Love frequency. There is no lack. Only Abundance, Love, Peace, and Joy.

    - You see life as an expression

    - Life is Divine Love

    - You have pure Spiritual Wisdom

    - You no longer strive for your Purpose as you now know in your Heart and Soul that you are 'it', the Divine spark of Universal Love

    - You live from a space of Humility and Grace

Gandhi and Mother Theresa were vibrating at this level when living their Life Purpose and Living their embodied Legacy.

Which stage do you feel you are at, mostly, in your life right now? If you're not sure, try asking yourself the following questions to get clarity.

1. Do you feel a sense of lack or scarcity?

2. Or do you feel a sense of abundance and prosperity?

3. Are you living from a mindset of fear or love?

4. Do you live in gratitude or envy?

5. Are you forgiving or do you hold a grudge?

6. Do you feel a sense of inner peace no matter what is going on around you?

7. Do you trust that everything will work out for the best for all?

8. Do you live in flow or force?

9. What is your life and who are you in it?

10. What is the legacy you are creating and living and showing by example, and is it empowering?

From here I invite you to check in on yourself regularly, becoming more aware and in tune with where you are living from and how you can move up and stay in a higher vibration. Remember we are human and we are going to move through these different stages at different times. A question we might ask ourselves is, *How can we elevate for the greater good?*

CHAPTER 22

Live Your Vision, Live Your Legacy

"Our deepest fear is not that we are inadequate. Our deepest fear is that we are powerful beyond measure. It is our light, not our darkness that most frightens us. We ask ourselves, Who am I to be brilliant, gorgeous, talented, fabulous? Actually, who are you not to be?"

— *Marianne Williamson*

Before we move into the main event of this chapter, in which we will begin the expansive process of activating and connecting with your Vision, I would like to ask:

What does the word 'legacy' mean to you?

For some people, their legacy is a far-away thing, and not something to consider or contemplate right now. The dictionary defines it as, "Something like a monetary gift or property that is handed down from the past". To me this is outdated and heavy. It's also potentially purely materialistic and ego-based.

I'd like us to reframe the concept of what a legacy can be so that it's less of something that we leave, and more something that we can *live*. Right now.

We live our legacy when we live our Vision. It's about how people feel with us, how we leave them feeling, and the impact we are having day by day, week by week. Living it and embodying it now in this moment and every moment.

Every day is an opportunity to inspire, to create connections, and use your gifts, your talents, and abilities for the greatest good. Now *that* is a life worth living. *That* is a life that will fill your Heart and the Hearts of others with wonder and curiosity. And what a legacy that is! Now this is cosmic Elemental Abundance.

Are you ready to connect to your authentic path and start creating from your Inner Compass, your Inner Wisdom?

It's time to connect to your Vision and start aligning to your journey, knowing that how you show up everyday matters.

I have used the following exercise both for myself and with my clients. It's a great one to do when you're looking to start something new, and when you want to get that clarity of Vision we discussed when we began exploring the AIR principle. This process has worked brilliantly in workshops I've run that have ended with creating a Vision board. You might just be pleasantly surprised when you set your intention to make what you discover a reality.

This exercise invites you to intuitively create and develop an idea, project, or concept, then later you can look for the practical linear things you need to do.

YOUR VISION QUEST

The purpose of this process is to set your Inner compass towards your Big Vision, tuning into your Inner Wisdom, and taking the smoothest possible route.

This process is inspired and influenced by the teachings of Reverend Michael Beckwith and his *Life Visioning Process*.

It's a reflective and meditative process which requires you to go inwards, but it's an excellent idea to have a pen and paper ready to journal the insights you'll gain from this process.

To begin, please drop into your Heart Activation and breathe from your Heart. (Chapter 4)

Next, ask yourself the questions below. Take your time. Linger on each one for a few minutes to allow the space for inspiration to drop in. Be open to any sensations, colours, shapes, images, feelings, and ideas that arise with each question. There is no need to focus on the how, just be open to receiving the insights.

With your eyes closed, set your positive intention to be open to guidance, and be ready to receive the magic of inspiration. This is about looking for the inspiration and guidance to lead you forward.

Here are the questions.

1. What is the highest and best idea for my life right now?

(You can make this specific about a project, activity, your legacy, or a particular opportunity, or keep it open.)

2. What is seeking to emerge during this chapter in my life?

3. What must I become to allow this Vision to unfold?

4. What are the gifts, abilities, and talents that I bring to this Vision?

5. What must I release and let go of to make room for the greater good?

(This might include outdated beliefs, forgiveness, old behaviours, or an unhelpful mindset.)

6. What must I embrace and accept to allow this Vision to unfold?

7. What have I not realised?

8. What else do I need to know in this moment?

To end the process, put your hands on your Heart and breathe through it, feeling gratitude for what has, or hasn't, come through for you. Feel as if your Vision is already real right now and you are ready to step into the best version of yourself.

Take a deep breath in and exhale with a sigh as you open your eyes to journal what has emerged.

When journaling, let the words or images flow without analysing them or getting caught up in the 'how'. Trust the process and feel into the energy and gratitude of this. So often I find that when we become true to our visions by believing in them and ourselves, we can be surprised by what is already so easily in reach, realising what we already have that can support us on our quest. Have fun with this.

You may choose to create a Vision Board with images, words, and phrases inspired by the insights or ideas you've received.

Importantly, be open for more intuitive hits as the following days unfold.

The magic of this practice is that you can do it to allow a Big Vision to emerge and rise up for you, or you can do it to get guidance and clarity on anything you are already creating in your life, such as a long-term project or a business idea. Keep dropping back in to see what is 'alive' for you to do each day to realise your Vision. In this way, you're creating something akin to a 'living Vision board', rather than a static or set-in-stone one.

The Vision Quest process is also great for keeping and fuelling the Vision which we will action in the FIRE principle. We'll be lighting sparks in the Hope Map exercise in Chapter 27, and then you'll continue to fan the flames throughout the rest of the book.

CHAPTER 23

The Best Version of You

"The more you see yourself as what you'd like to become, and act as if what you want is already there, the more you'll activate those dormant forces that will collaborate to transform your dream into your reality."

— Wayne W. Dyer

If you're being honest, where would you say your thoughts are, most of the time? Are you mostly living in the present, or are you often thinking about the past, and lamenting over all the mistakes and missteps you've ever made?

And even when you are in the here and now, what are you focusing on?

Too many of us inadvertently focus on what we *don't* want instead of what we *do* want. We notice what's missing in our lives instead of what we have. We live from a sense of scarcity and lack instead of opportunity and possibility.

Let us look to the horizon and set our course towards our dream as we embody our best possible life now.

Let us look to the future and call on that beautiful life we'll create by BEing that future version of ourselves in the present moment.

In positive psychology, it's been discovered that optimistically looking to the future can help us discover new pathways to navigate as we open up our awareness to the field of infinite possibilities. This practice offers some pretty amazing gains by increasing our mood, boosting our confidence, increasing academic and workplace outcomes, and improving our personal well-being.

Be aware that looking to your future desires and dreams is not an invitation to get down about your present circumstances. You are looking to expand into this future Vision, to allow it to pull you forward positively and guide you to make the choices you need to make that will support you on your quest to create your best life.

We can tap into this future now by calling on our Best Possible Self and what we would be like if we were 100% safe, and weren't afraid. What would your life be like?

BEST POSSIBLE SELF EXERCISE

This exercise is very profound, very deep, and therefore it's one which really lends itself to being heard rather than read. If you'd like me to talk you through it, you'll find a recording in our community group, here: www.ionarussell.com/elemental-circle

Begin by contemplating the notion of your 'Best Possible Self'. It's you at your Highest, your Happiest, your most Peaceful. It's you when you're inspired, loving and joyful.

Consider what your Best Possible Self is doing in your future. What are you creating? How are you living? What is inspiring you? What is having the greatest impact in your life and the lives of those around you?

Remember it's not just you who will benefit from this future you are creating, it is those who know you, maybe your children if you have them, perhaps your partner, your friends, and those that you will work with on this Vision to live your legacy now.

Now make yourself comfortable and have some relaxing uplifting positive music playing in the background. Make sure you have your journal to write in after you've completed the visualisation we are about to do.

1. Turn off any distractions and sit comfortably. Drop into your Heart Activation.

2. Start to imagine a future scene in front of you. It might help to imagine this playing out on a movie screen. You can choose if you want to see it six months, twelve months, or two years from now. Feel into what is most exciting and intriguing for you.

3. See everything as if it has turned out well for you.

4. What is it that shows you that everything is going well for you?

5. What are the feelings and known senses? You might see or sense that you're prosperous, abundant, inspired, peaceful, adventurous, magical, free, easy, joyful, loving, strong, confident, magnetic.

6. Notice what you are doing. Who are you with? Where are you?

7. What are you wearing? What are the people around you doing? If there is no one with you that is perfect too. This is all about you.

8. What do you hear? What do you see? What aromas do you notice, if any?

9. Notice the colours and textures around you.

10. Breathe this scene in, deeply. Feel it, sense it, and know it throughout your entire BEing. Feel it radiating from your Heart and permeating every cell of your body.

11. When you feel this deeply in your Heart, I now want you to step into this scene and stand in your own shoes looking out of your own eyes. Be in the scene. If you are already in the scene fully embodied as You then continue to integrate.

12. Turn up the colours, clarify the sights and sounds, and make this whole experience vivid and clear. Amplify it and turn up the dial. Turn your magic all the way up.

13. Breathe into this for a few moments and then when you are ready, put your hands to your Heart, smile, breathe deeply for three breaths, and when you're ready, open your eyes.

Journal on this experience, noticing how this felt emotionally.

- Are you inspired and motivated?

- What new possibilities has this opened up for you?

I invite you to visualise, connect to and step into this scene of your Best Possible Self every day. You might find some of your insights overlap with those you gained during the Vision Quest exercise, and that's okay. For some, the Vision Quest is about a felt sense of Source insight, whereas Best Possible Self is more about them as the individual. Have fun and play with these processes. The possibilities are limitless. There are no rules — you get to reinvent what's possible for you. This is all about you.

You could create a playlist to go along with this process if that lifts you up and inspires you.

I tend to do the Vision Quest in silence, treating is a meditative practice, but with Best Possible Self I prefer a more dynamic energy and listen to uplifting music. Feel into what feels right for you. There are many roads to Rome, as they say!

CHAPTER 26

Reflections & Suggestions: Air Element

1. You can find out more about Reverend Michael Bernard Beckwith with a quick online search. The first book of his that I read is *Life Visioning: A Transformative Process for Activating Your Unique Gifts and Highest Potential* published by Sounds True Inc. At the time of writing this book he also runs online workshops with The Shift Network, has a show on Gaia TV, is featured with Mindvalley, and has his own Agape University where you can learn more about his work and Life Visioning. If the opportunity to attend Agape ever arises, I strongly encourage you to go. There are lots of versions of the questions asked in the Vision Quest process in many other New Thought communities. A little search online will open up lots of doors to exploring levels of consciousness, or frequency of consciousness.

2. Further reading on concepts of energy and consciousness can be found in Power vs Force written by David R. Hawkins, published by Hay House. There is a wonderful illustration of the map of consciousness showing the vibrational energy frequencies moving up from force to power, going all the way from shame up to enlightenment.

3. Discovering Marianne Williamson's book *A Return to Love* (published by Harper Thorsons) marked a pivotal moment in my life and my own journey of me returning home to myself when I was 42. This is ten years ago now. A lot has happened in that time … and a lot more will happen in the decades to come.

4. Also check out *The Power of Intention* by Dr. Wayne Dyer, published by Hay House.

5. The research on how repeatedly using the 'Best Possible Self' exercise and writing out our goals improves our well-being and boosts our mood, happiness levels, optimism, hope, coping skills, and positive expectations about the future is covered in a couple of articles. 1) King. 2001. "The Health Benefits of Writing about Life Goals"; 2) Meevissen, Peters, Albert 2011 "Become more optimistic by imagining a best possible self. Effects of a two-week intervention" and Sheldon & Lyubomirsky. 2006 "How to increase and sustain positive emotion: The effects of expressing gratitude and visualizing best possible selves."

6. For anyone sceptical of the impact and amazing effects of actively using visualisation, in the study mentioned above titled "Become more optimistic by imagining a best possible self: Effects of a two-week intervention" they found that 'imaginary and visualizations involve deeper cognitive processing as compared to verbalization or writing'. I first heard about this study through the course with PPCA by Niyc Pidgeon and Mel Deague (see Chapter 20 #7) So let's all add visualisation into our daily lives. What have we got to lose? Nothing... but we have everything to gain.

7. If you're yet to join our community group, why not glide in today and share your experience with the Best Possible Self exercise? We'd love to hear from you. www.ionarussell.com/elemental-circle

PART 5: FIRE

Alignment

CHAPTER 27

The Fire Principle

FIRE represents the Energy behind Inspired Prepared Action, a fuel for Transformation, representing your Personal Power, and Inner Strength. It is the fire in your belly, the fire that moves us and fuels the action that must occur for anything to be created. And Abundant Creation requires bright, flaming Fires to Manifest.

It's time to ignite your Mission. You are a Creatrix and you are here to live with Impact, Joy, Ease and Prosperity. When you ignite the FIRE within You — the FIRE which supports Self-motivation — you will be inspired to take Aligned Action and transform Your life.

> *"She woke up one day and decided to set her life on fire: to go up in flames if necessary. To live the life she was born to live."*
>
> *— Lynn Bartle*

To truly evoke this element, we must ask what brings the FIRE to our Dreams, and discover what can turn tinder into a beautiful bonfire of bounty.

Well, it may not be what or how you think! The 'Science' of fire tells us it requires three things to exist: Fuel, Heat, Oxygen, or as I like to describe it here:

- Fuel – Your Reason Why

- Heat – Energy of Doing

- Oxygen – Recognition and Reward

And now, my dear reader, the time is upon us to ignite YOUR mission, fuel YOUR visions, and activate YOUR living legacy. You have a burning quest written across your Heart, flowing through your Soul, that only you can birth into the world.

So, first let's create a plan. The act of planning (which is just a fancy word for 'thinking through in advance') can make your goals, ambitions, and aspirations actualise in the world, for without a plan we are rudderless and at the mercy of the ever-changing currents.

I know, I know... "I'm too magical for planning", I hear you cry! You know, sometimes that resistance to having a strategy of any kind has led me to jump ship into the storm — quite literally out of the frying pan and into the fire. So many times I have found myself leaping between trying, wanting, striving, working hard, forcing outcomes, trying to make everything be perfect with the perfect outline, perfect results ... only to then end up stuck in procrastination, overwhelm, and honestly just being feckin' exhausted. Burn out, anyone?

Neither of these polar opposite ways of BEing has ever served me or the greater good — and they won't serve you, either.

Balance is the key. When we create from balance, with ease and flow, we navigate the changing tides with the effortlessness of a seasoned weather witch, or a salty pirate, adjusting the sails on the southerly summer's breeze in the Caribbean.

It is good to have something to aim for, something that your internal compass is pointing you to, like the stars on the horizon guiding you home.

I became more at ease with goal-setting when I realised having goals could be less about getting results in an A-to-B-to-C fashion and more about using goals as the fuel to inspire and drive me forward, so I could grow. Goals for me are not a stagnant destination, but are ever-evolving growing sparks, igniting each other towards a higher heightened glowing flame and I call these Goals with Soul.

Think of your potential goals in an expansive way, so that they are part of your path, and not the final destination. If we hold onto our goals and try to achieve them at all costs, we're in danger of being too rigid, and too narrow in our view of what's possible for us and what can bring us joy and success.

When we're too laser-focused we block out other opportunities, ideas, and inspirations. For example, if your end goal is to own a Ford Fiesta and you get so intent on that goal, you'll close yourself off to anything beyond that price range, and you'll close yourself off to the possibility of owning a Rolls Royce or Mercedes Benz.

So let's get a little more focused on identifying our goals with Soul. The technique I'm about to share is the one I use to approach my goals now. It only took me 51 years to find this! I'm so glad I did. It's called Hope Mapping, and it's a Positive Psychology process developed by Charles Synder.

HOPE MAPPING

I like Hope Mapping, its basically planning for believers. This process can be used for anything which has a future focus. You can even use it to do the things you'd rather avoid. I had one client who used this process to get creative and inspired enough to submit her taxes. But it works just as well for those Big Dreams, and I always encourage you to Dream Big! In fact, when it comes to the Big Stuff, let's call your goals 'Soul Goals' or 'Goals With Soul'. We are here to accomplish greatness so let's make our goals mean something to us.

As psychologist and renowned hope researcher Charles Snyder et al. (2002, p. 269) stated so eloquently:

"A rainbow is a prism that sends shards of multi-coloured light in various directions. It lifts our spirits and makes us think of what is possible. Hope is the same – a personal rainbow of the mind."

We can all use a little rainbow of hope in our lives to guide us forwards to the horizon of our dreams.

I find this process very practical in providing me with actional pathways to getting something accomplished. Remember we are here to take action; some days that action will be like a warm simmer, and other times it will be more like you're running on rocket fuel. Whichever way it is — action is always forward motion. We're going to explore the power of action in the coming chapters, so see this exercise as a building block to get you clearer on what action you can take to keep your fire burning.

You'll need a piece of paper and a pen for this process. Please see the example in your community circle at www.ionarussell.com/elemental-circle

1. The magic of Hope Mapping is you can use it for something exciting or something you've just 'got' to do. Not everything is high vibe and sexy with sparkle dust! Sometimes we just have things we just gotta do. Whether it's a Soul Goal or not, write it clearly at the top of your page, leaving space underneath to add a sentence or two later.

2. Next, draw three columns and title them: Actions, Obstacles, and Pathways.

3. Now in the Actions column, list several action steps you can take towards your goal.

4. Review each of the action steps and for each action list an obstacle in the Obstacle column.

5. Drop into your Heart Space and let's get creative. What are the ways of overcoming or circumnavigating the obstacles? These are your pathways: write these in the third column. You may come up with completely new ways of moving forward, thinking of new action steps as you go, in which case write the new action steps in column one and work your way through the process again looking for any obstacles. Again, identify the pathways to overcome the new obstacles.

6. As you consider your pathways, who might be able to support you on each one? This might mean working with an accountability partner. We all need support in our lives, no one is an island. Together we are stronger.

7. Why is this goal important to you? Perhaps you might want to consider who else benefits from this goal. When you identify your 'Why' add this as the extra sentence or two at the top of the page where you left that space.

To complete this process, I invite you to take some time to visualise and really imagine what following your pathways and reaching your Soul Goal will look like and feel like. Visualise this daily and allow yourself to feel as if you have reached your Soul Goals.

I further invite you to hold yourself accountable by sharing this. Who can you ask to hold you accountable?

This process can be applied to just about any decision, ambition, desire, or future-focused goal. Have fun and feel it real.

Note: If you'd like to dive deeper into Hope theory after experiencing Hope mapping, please look up Snyder 2002, 'Hope theory: Rainbows in the mind', in the journal Psychological Inquiry.

CHAPTER 28

Mining Your Fuel for the Fire

*"Our deepest fear is not that we are inadequate. Our deepest
fear is that we are powerful beyond measure. It is our light,
not our darkness that most frightens us. We ask ourselves,
'Who am I to be brilliant, gorgeous, talented, fabulous?'
Actually, who are you not to be? You are a child of God. Your
playing small does not serve the world. There is nothing
enlightened about shrinking so that other people won't feel
insecure around you. We are all meant to shine, as children
do. We were born to make manifest the glory of God that
is within us. It's not just in some of us; it's in everyone. And
as we let our own light shine, we unconsciously give other
people permission to do the same. As we are liberated from
our own fear, our presence automatically liberates others."*

— *Marianne Williamson*

When you tried the Hope Mapping exercise at the end of chapter 27, how easy was Step 7 for you, where I asked you to write your 'Why' at the top of the page?

Often, 'Why' is the hardest question to answer. It can take a little excavating to uncover, but when we do tap into it, our Why becomes our fuel, essential for starting our Fire AND keeping it burning.

Whether you have a sense of your Why or not, for the Hope Mapping process or for any other Soul Goals that are calling to you, I invite you to take some time to explore this area, going deeper than you may have already.

Uncovering our Whys can be a little confronting, because getting to the deeper Why takes moving beyond two potentially daunting obstacles: the fear of our own power, and the realisation that there are infinite possibilities before us.

We may also fear being seen, being judged as worthy or not, and even being too fulfilled, whole and Abundant. Not to mention all those other gremlins that can pop up when we are driven to change the trajectory of our lives, or the lives of others, in some small or big way.

Let me talk to those gremlins. They are sneaky little creatures and all they need is some love and reassurance. To paraphrase Marianne Williamson: we and our gremlins are either coming from a place of Fear or Love.

I am not immune to the odd gremlin myself. In writing this book I had a moment two days ago as I started to go through the final edits, wondering, *Why am I doing this, who am I to do this, who even wants to read this...* I even shed a couple of tears of overwhelm.

And then I took my own advice shared here with you in this book. I dropped into the Heart Activation with my conscious breathing and reflected on three good things in the last 24 hours. Then I brought into my imagination my Big Vision, and my scary AF next Quest (that's a process I'll be sharing with you in the final chapter) and I connected to my Why with my Heart. I did all this whilst barefoot on the grass in my garden.

BOOM.

I started to feel my Heart warm and glow and grow as I connected to Mother Earth.

I'd had a wobble and then I got back on track. I reached out to a couple of supportive friends and shared. I leaned into their support and pulled up my chair to the computer and felt into what I wanted to say to you in this chapter.

Too often we try to smother down, suppress, and ignore our feelings: those negative gremlins who are just trying to keep us safe by keeping us in the familiar safety zone. As 'they' say — it's better the devil you know. Well, no it isn't!

As with the inner child work, I asked what I/ the gremlins/we needed in this moment, and I just listened and Loved every worry and fear that came up. This is Inner Power at play with Love, and to Love, all the aspects of us, warts and all makes make us dynamite.

Self-doubt is okay. You're okay as you are. Changes take time and yet choosing not to change anything can cost us something greater than time, it can cost us our Life Force, our Essence for living, and our expansive Heart.

You are here for greatness and the world needs you to birth your Vision. Remember I said earlier that you have a burning mission written across your Heart, flowing through your Soul, that only you can birth into the world?

It's true. Shall we dive deeper, and find more of your fuel?

WHAT IS THE FUEL, YOUR 'WHY' THAT IGNITES YOU?

Sometimes I'm an advocate of the phrase, "First thought best thought", and other times I disagree. And this might be one of those times. Bear with me. Often, when we're asked a question, our first response of might be what we think we should say, or what society thinks is the 'right' answer.

So when I ask you the following question, I invite you to go beyond any initial obvious answers. Whatever your answer is, I want it to be a full-body riveting one! One that makes you go, "Feck YES! That's it!"

Here's the question:

What is your Why?

By which I mean: What's the big reason, driving motivation, or raging FIRE behind what you hope to create and be in this world?

This doesn't have to be something so big that it would solve world hunger, cure cancer, or end homelessness. All of these are amazing quests — but only if they are yours. If they're not, and they're someone else's Vision, their why is fuelling them — but that doesn't mean it has to fuel you.

Your driving force is personable to you.

It's okay if you don't know your Why just yet, it can take some digging. Quite often the route of our Why is tied into something we went through as a child, something we have overcome as an adult, or something that has inspired us or empowered us along the way.

I have some explorative questions for you to play with that will help you to find more of your fuel. After you've done a little, or a lot, of investigating, the idea is you'll be able to form a Why statement, in your own words, expressed in whatever way is natural to you.

Start by looking back over your life at the pivotal moments. It can be helpful to do this by drawing out a timeline. Literally, on a piece of paper draw a line from birth to now and mark the pivotal moments. These can be highs as well as lows, uplifting experiences as well as speed bumps, and challenges you overcame or learned from.

Your pivotal moments could include things like: that moment you found out your parents were divorcing and felt different to all your friends' families; the time you won the spelling bee and were celebrated; the time you were heartbroken; the time you fell in Love; the volunteer work you did; the worst job you ever had which made you realise you didn't want to be in that sector; the highs and lows of traveling through Tibet. You get the idea!

- Do you see a common thread through these pivotal moments? What is it?

- What have you overcome?

- What has made you feel the most alive, most motivated?

- What/who has inspired you?

- What do you never want someone to experience?

- What do you want someone to experience?

- What are you willing to struggle for?

- What will you not stand for? Personally, and in the World?

- What do you stand for? Personally, and in the World?

- What is important to you?

- What are you a stand for? Meaning, what will you not tolerate? What is it you are passionate about ending? What don't you want anyone, or anything, else to have to endure?

- Who are you, and who do you want to be?

To each of these questions as you answer them, ask How? Or Why?

Keep asking and going deeper with this. Here's an example:

- What is important to you?

   a. And why is that important to you?

   b. And why?

   c. What else can you tell me about this?

   d. And what is important about that?

You see the general idea. It might help to have someone ask you these questions or you can come and join the free community and membership site I have created to support you on your Journey. This is a free space for you to dive deeper into this work. www.ionarussell. com/elemental-circle

- Keep going and exploring your Why with these questions:

- What do people come to you for support with? Write/Tell me more

- What are you naturally good at? (Skills, abilities, gifts, zone of genius)

- How do you influence others? In what way?

- Who else gains from your work, project, or purpose? And in what way?

- What are your best relationships based on?

- What is your personal philosophy? How are you living it?

Now consider what areas you want to improve or change in your life or the lives of others. You can choose multiple or add ones, not on the list. There are no rules.

- Health

- Happiness

- Mental wellbeing

- Relationships

- Wealth

- Social or political policy

- Spiritual Growth

- Eco Culture

- Green living

- Children

Next, explore and contemplate:

- What does living an extraordinary life mean for you?

- Why is this important?

- Who is important to you?

- What problem do you hate to see in the world?

- What value do/will you create?

- What is your unique brilliance?

- What comes easy to you, that you do better than 90% of the rest of the world?

- If you knew you were 100% safe, and money was no issue what would you do?

I get that I've just given you a lot of questions to ponder. Take your time and if it feels draining rather than igniting at any time come back to it later.

Quite often, our BIG why is hidden in plain sight, and when we unveil it, it becomes our secret sauce or our magic rocket fuel that will lift us up and drive us when the gremlins might try to knock us down.

When you look back on whatever has arisen for you in the chapter to weave together your Why, you might come up with a paragraph rather than just a why statement. Some of the people I work with have written this out as a whole A4 sheet of paper! Rather than an elevator pitch, it's an expression of their aligned Vision with the deeper connection to their why and with who. I will share my own version into our free community here www.ionarussell.com/elemental-circle

These above questions are inspired by my work, along with processes I've been through and within PPCA.

CHAPTER 29

Fanning the Flames with Action

*"Whatever you can do or dream you can begin it. Boldness
has genius, power, and magic in it."*

— *Johann Wolfgang von Goethe*

Now you're fuelled up with your why, let's amplify those flames by adding heat to your FIRE. Heat comes from doing, and in doing we find more of our power as we take aligned and inspired action. In action we build momentum, and our fires burn brighter.

Taking action requires that we be bold. Armed with our plan we are inspired and prepared. We know what we want to create, and we have our Why to call on to keep the flames alive.

But I'd be remiss if I didn't mention that as we build up momentum and illuminate our path with all we've learned so far, there will be moments when we may doubt ourselves, our resolve may fade, and we feel that we have to force the outcomes. Whenever we feel the need to apply force we're using precious energy, and our reserves — which we have been stoking to keep fuelled up with our work from the earlier chapters — diminish.

This is where you must work in flow, combining the willingness to live from your Heart and an acceptance that there will be rises and falls in the temperatures of your Inner Fires and burning Mission. Flowing without forcing.

How do you know when you're forcing something? By how you feel. When you're living from your Inner Power and your True Authentic Self, you feel invincible, Self-sustaining, and there's a strong sense you're grounded in your Purpose and Vision. You have radical, exquisite confidence that feels gentle rather than overpowering.

So what is it that changes the tide and pulls us away from that place of Power? What keeps us in resistance, unable to take action?

It is fear.

Fear can show up as a lack of self-belief, a sense of unworthiness, or a lack of confidence. It might make us fall back into old patterns and programming, and revert to old behaviours. The fact is, changing the course of our lives for the greater good will bring up fear, and I'd love to share with you this one beautiful truth that can set you free:

Fear and excitement feel the same — and when we know that, we get to choose where we operate from.

Truly understanding this can be the key to untethering you and overcoming any fears you have about taking action towards your Mission.

Let me tell you how I learned this. The first time I was hired to speak on stage at an event I was so excited because this was everything I'd been working towards; I knew this opportunity was going to be a game changer for me. But the week before the event, nerves set in — big time. And as the days counted down, the nervousness and the accompanying self-doubt only increased.

The night before the event I wanted to call in sick, to cancel. Who the heck was I to do this? What would my peers think? What if I sucked? What if no one came? What if I failed? All of these fearful thoughts swam through my mind, making it hard to focus.

To make things worse, I'd been procrastinating and hadn't settled on exactly what I wanted to talk about. The fear was really kicking in and holding me back from moving forward.

That morning, my nerves were jangled, and I was in hyper mode. The temptation to cancel was huge, but I realised my Vision for my future was greater. And if I wanted to keep sailing to that future, cancelling just wasn't an option — that would kill my career and reputation quicker than a bad song at the Eurovision Song Contest.

I was to speak to a room of 100 at the Wellbeing Festival here in Edinburgh. This was my next Big Scary AF step toward my dreams. And I didn't want to do it... but I knew I had to. I reminded myself this was an epic opportunity and just what I'd been visualising and working towards. This was me adding more fuel (more of my why) to my FIRE, and that allowed me to turn up the heat by taking action and leaning into the fear.

And so, I dropped in and showed up as myself, even wearing my faithful Converse trainers. What you see is what you get with me, and this is how I felt comfortable that day.

The audience was brilliant, the room was full, the laughter loud, the presentation went over a treat and I got into such a flow that I was literally flying off the stage.

Now that was a natural high of EPIC proportions!

It was a quantum leap outside my comfort zone.

This was the beginning of a new chapter for me, and I use that experience as a reminder that every time I feel fear because now I know the following fundamental truths:

- It didn't kill me last time.

- Fear and excitement feel the same in the body.

- Magic happens beyond the comfort zone.

- I actually enjoy leaning into fear

I realise on reflection that the fear of *not doing* something is quite often the driving force of growth and expansion for me (maybe that's why I love skydiving, but that's a story for another day). When I realised this about myself, an opening was created.

I invite you to think about your own relationship with fear, but do begin gently. Ease into the aspect of fear so as not to overwhelm your nervous system. Come and share your musings, insights, wonderings on fear in our community group. Whatever you find, it's all perfect. There is no right way or wrong way. It's for you to recognise where you are in your relationship to fear, so you can move through it.

Stepping into your big Vision and living your legacy will mean doing things that scare you. My advice is to never cancel on yourself, your dreams, and the people you will inspire and impact.

If I'd cancelled, would I even be here right now writing this book to you? I very much doubt it.

When fear, procrastination and self-sabotaging doubts kick in, know that magic is about to happen. You have to step outside your comfort zone to grow and being aware of this will give you focus.

Now would be a good time to reflect on the Hope Mapping exercise from Chapter 27. Part of that process involved identifying actions you need to take to move towards your goal. What can you do this week, or even today, to move you forward?

If you sense it would help you, create a support system of people to cheer you on and hold you accountable. Always drop back into your big Vision and tap into why you are doing whatever is conjuring that fear. Keep coming back to your big Vision and tuning into it.

I remind all my one-to-one clients that when they undertake the level of transformation we're going for here, they will want to quit, they will think they've done enough of the inner work, and they will want to hide. Each and every client has had these moments at least once in our time working together. They have me for support and to call them forward and hold space for them. Please surround yourself with people who inspire you and will hold you to a bigger Vision.

The right people around us will support us emotionally and energetically. They want you to succeed, they will feel like home, and they will hold your Vision for you and with you when you are questioning yourself.

As we move on to our next exercise, I invite you to take a moment to imagine that you will live to be 100. What is it that you want people to remember you for? Let's explore this in greater depth.

WRITE YOUR OWN EPITAPH

This can be an emotional exercise, but it's a powerful one. Again, this one is best experienced via the free audio in our online group. www.ionarussell.com/elemental-circle

It might seem unusual to think about your own epitaph but going to the end of our lives and stepping back to view where we are now from that perspective can ignite incredible insights. It can help us adjust our trajectory and inspire us to see the changes we are here to make. After all, when you stand from a point in the future, you can look back and see how you got there.

I invite you to have positive uplifting music playing whilst doing this exercise.

Have your journal handy for after you have finished this exercise.

1. Sitting comfortably, tune into and activate your Heart. For the rest of this exercise, I invite you to keep your hands on your Heart.

2. Imagine you have lived a beautiful, loving, and magnificent life. Have a sense of this in your Heart.

3. Your life is complete, and you have the opportunity to write your own epitaph.

4. I want you to consider what it is that you would like to have written here.

5. What would you like someone to say about you at the celebration of your life?

6. How would you like other people to remember you?

7. How would you like people to feel when they think about you?

8. What memories do you want them to recall of your life?

9. What's important for you to have done?

10. What's important for you to have been?

11. How is it important for you to have lived?

12. What is it you would like to be remembered for?

13. What is it that lets you know you lived a good and happy life?

14. With your hands on your Heart, take three deep breaths, and sigh on each out-breath

Open your eyes

- Journal on this experience and what came through for you

- What would you like to be remembered for?

- From today, what moves the needle most for you towards that epitaph being written? What can you do this coming week? Month? And year?

- What actions will you take first?

I hope you have found it useful to reflect back on your life and how you want to live it. We so often look forward when planning. A lot of clients do this exercise and find that it's not the stuff they had, it's the people in their lives, and how they made them feel that they value the most. It's not about how much time they had, but what they did with it.

There is no right or wrong way for this to unfold. Some people realise that what they've been focusing on isn't important to them when viewing life from this perspective and they make some amazing inspiring changes. Others are happy with how their life is. Others become emotional and realise they are veering away from what they originally intended with their life, their relationships, their careers, and so forth. Whatever this exercise taps into, may it be illuminating for you.

CHAPTER 30

The Combustion = Fuel + Heart + Oxygen (Igniting Your Why)

"I came to set fire to the earth. And I am watchful that the fire grow. May the fire of love grow in our hearts. May the fire of transformation glow in our movements. May the fire of purification burn away our sins. May the fire of justice guide our steps. May the fire of wisdom illuminate our paths. May the fire that spreads over the Earth never be extinguished."

— Paulo Coelho

Are you feeling all fired up? Now it is time to light the world up with your Vision. It is now time to tune in and connect to the Inner Wisdom in your Soul and ignite your Vision, your Dharma, your Life Purpose.

"Catch Fire, Do Something, Get Excited by Finding Your Purpose In Life."

— Steve Harvey

You get to choose how to live your Purpose. You create your big Vision to live your Legacy in every moment, every day. Remember that your Legacy is who you are and how you show up every day, day in and day out.

You are here to step into your power and live a full and free life, packed with possibility, unbridled fun, and the kind of experiences that only YOU can call into existence.

This is your journey, and your dance, after all. We have covered everything from clearing space to setting intentions, to tuning into your superpower of intuition and activating your big Vision. You have begun the process of being fully connected into your earthly Self and your Higher Self, through being rooted in Mother Earth and the joy of this life you are here to live. The philosophies, practices, and exercises in this book were all offered as a way to bring you back home to yourself and the Truth of who you are and what you are capable of. It is all connected: EARTH, WATER, AIR, FIRE, You, and Source. There is no separation. You get to dance the dance of your Soul's Purpose.

"There is no fire like passion, No crime like hatred, No sorrow like separation, No sickness like hunger, And no joy like the joy of freedom."

— *Gautama Buddha*

Rather than having a separate section of reflections and suggestions as we have throughout the rest of the book, I now invite you to strike the match and light the FIRE in your belly, leaping into this new chapter of your life fully attuned to the vibration of your unique Abundance. I know from experience that no one does this alone so let's add some kindling to the FIRE, besides joining the community which is your free membership circle at www.ionarussell.com/elemental-circle, consider:

1. How will you keep yourself motivated and accountable?

2. Who is in your support network that you could join forces with?

-And-

3. Every day, will you ask yourself: what can I do today to fan the flames of my Abundant life?

FIND YOUR PEOPLE

We are born with an innate need to belong and be part of something bigger than us as individuals. It's the eternal quest we all go on in search of our people, a group of like-minded visionaries, creatives, wisdom keepers, and the new EARTH leaders. When they soar, we feel it in our hearts. We connect and are inspired. This is the oxygen to our FIRE.

I see this quest in my clients, in the people who attend my live and online events: this sense of coming home to feel safe and uplifted with others.

"Set your life on fire. Seek those who fan your flames."

— Rumi

If you can't find what you're looking for then create it — find your people, and when you do, I invite you to share from your Heart. You will inspire others, and these will be kindred Souls on this journey of Elemental Abundance for us all.

And of course, come and join the community that has been created for you. Come and join us, your fellow kindred souls on this journey through the Elements of Abundance in creating your Heart-Full Abundant life with ease, Prosperity, Passion and Pizazz.

THE SCARY AF BIG ASKS

Do you want to know what the dynamite, magical, and mysteriously zesty ingredients are that will spice up your manifestation cake of creation and awe?

Yes!

Are you ready to do something you've never done before?

Yes!

Are you ready to walk through the FIRE and break through the comfort barrier?

Yes

With three Yeses we are going to get this party started.

Yes, Yes, Yes!

It's time to embrace the Big Scary AF asks.

You might be wondering what the heck I'm talking about.

These are things you that the old version of you couldn't or wouldn't dare to ask for fear of judgment, for fear of a No, for fear of everyone will think I'm crazy.

My beautiful Wild Heart, you won't get to where you are needing to grow to if you keep doing the same things you did before. Nothing changes if you don't change the way you take action. And putting your scary AF asks out to the Universe — and to other people — ignites the change you were born to create.

If you don't ask those scary AF asks then basically it's a No — so what have you got to lose? You might just get a YES.

But wait, Iona, What are these BIG ASKS, and who am I asking? I hear you say.

The asking we're talking about here is about reaching out. It's about outwardly asking and approaching people who can help you. They might be able to connect you to someone who can assist you towards your goal, or they might just be the exact person you need to jump on board with you and make your Dream happen.

These Asks are about advancing the project, Vision, or idea forward and igniting the turbo-fuelled booster jets of creation to make it a reality.

You might want to begin by asking yourself, Who are the ten people I can approach who might just be ones to help make this happen?

Let's say you want to host your first women's circle, but you're nervous and worried no one will come. Even just inviting some women along might be scary enough for you. In this case, I'd advise you not to make the ten asks the ten women. Have this count as one ask. Another ask might be to approach a venue to host your event. But let's say you don't have the money to hire, so your next scary AF Ask is to present your idea to the venue in such a way that they feel aligned with your mission to support these women, and they're willing to either host your event for free or work out another way you can pay or contribute to their business.

Now, if any of this is easy for you to do, then this isn't your Scary AF Ask.

The Scary AF Asks are always outside your comfort zone.

Let me tell you about one of mine: I would love to interview or be interviewed by Russell Brand. So, a while ago, I buckled up, broke through my comfort zone, and reached out to him — and I got the nicest no I've ever received. But, around the same time, I also got an unexpected mind-blowing YES when I asked to interview Richard Rudd of the Gene Keys. (I mentioned him and the radio interview in Chapters 12 and 15. You can hear the interview on my website under 'radio shows and podcasts' tab.)

You will sometimes get a No and that's a good thing. View a No as something that is clearing the way and making room for other possibilities. Sometimes a 'No' will be 'not right now'. So I am still hoping one day I get to interview, or be interviewed by, Russell Brand.

You want a Yes to be a full and clear Yes.

You want a No to be clear as a No.

Also, clarify if a No is just not right now, or not yet.

No does indeed mean no, we know that. So I invite you to ask from your Heart and check with whoever you are asking if this is a No, never, or a not right now. Then ask, 'And how can I make this a yes for you?' Or perhaps they know someone else who might be interested and willing to help or work with you.

I have found, with my clients and for myself, that quite often we already have people in our network, in our communities, that are wanting and able to help, that have that connection that could change everything, that have the resources that will ignite your Vision and your Mission.

Talk about your Passion and your Vision to everyone, to the person you're standing next to in the supermarket queue, to the person waiting next to you in line for coffee, to the person you meet on a flight — essentially speak what you seek until what you seek is what you see. You will inspire, and you will build amazing connections and opportunities.

I know an amazing man, Matthew Liam Gardner (you can hear my interview with him on my website on my radio shows and podcasts speakers' corner) and I shall call him Brother Bear, who started a whole movement in Australia by following his inspired Heart and asking the big scary AF Asks. If you'd Love some inspired thoughts, ancient remembering, elders' stories from around the FIRE go check him out on Facebook.

I first heard about the Big Scary Asks as an approach from Brother Bear.

Only you can know what YOUR scary asks are. Remember I am here to guide, support, and hopefully inspire you to take your aligned action forwards on your Prosperous path — Activating your Vision, your Legacy, and raising the Vibration of this beautiful planet.

To Action: Come up with 10 Big Scary Asks and review them monthly.

At the end of each month reflect: Did I do them all? What were the results?

Remember the Big Scary AF Asks are personal to you. You will know in your body what is scary for you. A Scary Ask expands you out of your comfort zone and creates the impact and Vision you are here to make manifest.

If you don't ask, you don't get to create magic here on Earth. If you are worried that you will fall on your face and feel foolish, and that you're sure to get a No, I say to you: But what if you get a YES?

> *"There is freedom waiting for you, on the breezes of the sky.*
> *And you ask, "What if I fall?" Oh, but my darling, "What if you*
> *fly?"*
>
> — *Erin Hanson*

I promise you this is what will move the needle for you. This is a game changer.

And, what's beautiful about all of this, is you get to choose to say Yes to yourself, and select the opportunities that align in your path. When I was 42 and knew that my life had to change, I had no idea that this is what my life would look like ten years later. Even two years ago I couldn't have imagined my life like this. Dream the Dream, ask the scary AF asks, and keep moving forward.

I can't wait to witness your rise from the flames and see your light shining brighter than you ever imagined.

CHAPTER 31

The Final Key: The Elements in Harmony

"Success is loving life and daring to live it."

- Maya Angelou

As the book draws to a close, I invite you to consider the notion of balance and harmony. Just as nature relies on harmony and interconnectedness, so has our journey with the four elements. There is a reason we began with EARTH, before moving into WATER, AIR, and finally FIRE. That route paved the way for you to find your true Joy of Freedom, unlocking the four Keys, one by one, to your Elemental Abundance.

To be in balance in each of these areas is essential. Let's remind ourselves of how each element supports you to be Abundantly Successful in all areas of your life. Read through and recognise the journey, the flow, you have been on.

- EARTH: The Energy of your Open HEART. The Foundation of Being Grounded to the TRUTH of who you BE so that you are living in alignment with your Heart and Soul. Working with the Earth you grow grounded and rooted to the fullest expression of yourself, on your Prosperous Path and living from your Wealth Creation wellspring.

- WATER: The Energy of Healing your HEART to allow you to grow and move forward with your own Inner Wealth of Knowledge, no longer weighted down.

- AIR: The Energy of your Envisioned future allowing you to create your Elementally Abundant life, and to be living your Vision, not someone else's version of what you 'should' do

- FIRE: The Energy behind Inspired Prepared Action, your fuel for Transformation, Personal Power, and Inner strength. It is the Fire in your belly, the Fire that moves you and fuels the action that must occur for anything to be created. And Abundant Creation requires bright, flaming Fires to Manifest.

Having these four Elemental Keys in alignment and balance is what allows you to live at the NEW frontier of YOUR Creation. Again, we come back to balance. If you were to be dominant in one element, the harmony we seek becomes a discord. For example, you could be mastering the FIRE processes and taking Action, but feel confusion because you're not creating sustainable Abundance. This could be because you haven't healed through the WATER process, so you could be taking action out of spite or anger, or perhaps there's forgiveness work to be done. Or it could be that you haven't connected to your AIR element, and as such you might be living out someone else's Mission, someone else's Dream, and following their cookie-cutter model. Or if you haven't fully grounded into the EARTH element you will inevitably feel ungrounded and disconnected, and will be taking action out of harmony with who you really are, your fullest, most abundant expression.

I share this with you so you can be aware that we are all a work in progress, and that's perfect. Any time you feel out of balance, you now have these tools, awarenesses and practices to return to. They are evergreen. Please keep using them. Keep growing, learning, moving and burning so brightly. Come back to the ELEMENT of the truth of who you are every day.

So my dear Elemental reader, are you ready? You are an Intrepid, brave explorer on the leading edge of the new frontier.

The old ways of doing things haven't worked for you, and now you get to align with your Elements, and to create from your Abundant

HEART.

This is the moment to embrace your Highest timeline, and activate your Elements of Abundance of which you are here to manifest for the greatest good.

Will you take the Quantum leap of your Soul's Divine Purpose, the life you were born to create?

Are you ready to move from the disconnection of thinking you are separate, to knowing deeply that you are connected to everything and you are One with Source?

Is it time to call on the four elements of EARTH, WATER, AIR, and FIRE and really listen, really hear and create and finish the dance you spoke into existence on this EARTH?

Your Final Recommendations

1. Join your Free Community Circle at www.ionarussell.com/elemental-circle where you will find bonus material, PDF downloads, audio mediations, and videos from me to you.

2. Do the Daily Heart Activation to begin your day (listen to the guided audio version in our Elemental Community Circle)

3. Once a week do the Extended Heart Activation and connect with your natural Element.

4. Set an alarm for 11:11 (Chapter 13) every day and look back over the last 24 hours and notice any miracles, moments of gratitude, and intuitive hits you had. Make a note of them on your phone for ease, or a journal if this is convenient. Drop into your HEART space as you do this and make sure that you do this no matter what else is going on, for 60`seconds.

I was once asked by a mentor of mine, Hugh Gilbert, the following question, and it acted as a powerful wake-up call for me. So I'll ask it now of you.

Are you going to finish the Dance this time?

Only you can answer.

But I'm right here with you.

In the words of David Bowie: Let's Dance!

With Love and Gratitude

Iona xo

P.S I look forward to connecting with you in our free membership community where you can access all the bonus resources to unlock even more Elemental Abundance: www.ionarussell.com/elemental-circle

ACKNOWLEDGEMENTS

There are many who have assisted me along the pathway to this book's creation and completion.

First, my publishers and best friends Sean Patrick and Karen Mills-Alston of The Good House International Publishing. They have been my most confident cheerleaders, spiritual guides, and homing beacons. Always supporting the new directions this high-spirited process took me on. Providing me with new perspectives and guidance along the way.

I want to thank Richard Knight for his support over these last couple of years and cheering me on when I doubted myself, dusting me off when I fell over, and always bringing humour and fun to our collaborations, adventures, and misadventures. Once a maverick always a maverick.

One of the greatest lessons I've learned through the process of writing this book is the importance of having an empowering support network and for me, especially this past year, that showed up as the friendships, the collective wisdom, and outright bundle of sassiness that was my PPCA 'Quad-pod' ladies, Philippa Iles, Katie Cooper, and Faye Edwardes. And my good friend and personal trainer of mind body and soul, and dog walks, Laura Weavers.

This book has gone through many initial versions and more alterations than a wedding dress, and finally, and by no means least, I would like to thank my son Callum Russell for his patience in losing me to hours of research and writing.

BiO⌒

Iona Russell M.PPCA, Dip.C.Hyp

Born in the alternative lifestyle heyday of the early 70's near the UK's literary capital of Hay-on-Wye, being different and creative was in Iona Russell's blood. But with such freedom of spirit comes some confusion unless carefully guided. From wild child to postnatal depression, from free traveller to trapped in trauma, Iona had certainly "Lived" and experienced much by the time she settled in her ancestral homeland of Edinburgh over 2 decades ago.

But it was life and its lessons that gifted her with the passion and perseverance not only to align her own life authentically but to bring those gifts to the wider world through her writing and coaching. Guiding Wild Spirited Hearts, creatives, leaders, and entrepreneurs to create successful personally fulfilling and gloriously abundant lives on their terms, Iona is devoted to others living the life of impact and ease that they are born to live.

Originally pursuing her coaching career as a Practitioner in Neurolinguistic Programming (NLP), she has since explored and adopted a broader range of transformative methods, allowing greater flexibility and deeper intuitive connection with her clients, and accruing an impressive array of credentials and connections, as can be seen below.

A certified Positive Psychology Master Coach, Clinical Hypnotherapist, International multi best-selling Author, Speaker, and Radio presenter,

Iona has been described as the 'Wizard without the Illusions' by her clients and peers. She bridges the gap between evidence-based Positive Psychology and New Age Wisdom; aligning mind, body, and soul for self-empowered personal freedom, fulfilment, and Abundance.

Those who work with her get to break through their personal barriers, current performance plateaus, and money mindset patterns so they can confidently achieve their 'next level' dreams and aspirations.

With her specialist, 4 Elements Heart Activation (4E ♥ A) Methodology, a super-effective deep-dive solution-based process based on the scientific principles of neuroplasticity, and heart resonance Iona creates new empowering and energetic pathways that replace old unhelpful beliefs and behaviours; releasing the ties that bind. This leads to rapid, profound, and long-lasting transformation.

Now, through her international events and high-profile collaborations, Iona's flying high and currently working on developing additional group programmes that will mean even more people will gain the benefits of her knowledge, skills, and experience.

If you're ready to align and level up your life to absolute abundance, then visit www.ionarussell.com now, to find out more.

There is a free community membership for all the Elemental Abundance readers where you can share your insights, questions, musings, and inspirations. All the bonuses that expand the experience of reading this book will be hosted within the community, including PDFs, meditations, audios and videos... plus musings and contributions from Iona to help support you to go deeper. Come and join us here www.ionarussell.com/elemental-circle

BOOKS BY iONA RUSSELL

SOLO BOOKS

Making Waves (2020)

COLLABORATIVE BOOKS

Wild Hearted : Life Love and Liberation (2023)

A Woman's Voice is a Revolution (2023)

Shakti Farts & Belly Laughs (2022)

Goddess Empowered Entrepreneur (2022)

The Everyday Girls Guide to Living in Truth, Self-Love and Acceptance (2021)

Living Life Goddess Powered (2021)

Milton Keynes UK
Ingram Content Group UK Ltd.
UKHW020339160923
428761UK00011B/97